At the Margins

At the Margins

A Life in Biomedical Science, Faith,
and Ethical Dilemmas

D. Gareth Jones

RESOURCE *Publications* • Eugene, Oregon

AT THE MARGINS
A Life in Biomedical Science, Faith, and Ethical Dilemmas

Copyright © 2022 D. Gareth Jones. All rights reserved. Except for brief quotations in critical publications or reviews, no part of this book may be reproduced in any manner without prior written permission from the publisher. Write: Permissions, Wipf and Stock Publishers, 199 W. 8th Ave., Suite 3, Eugene, OR 97401.

Resource Publications
An Imprint of Wipf and Stock Publishers
199 W. 8th Ave., Suite 3
Eugene, OR 97401

www.wipfandstock.com

PAPERBACK ISBN: 978-1-6667-4471-2
HARDCOVER ISBN: 978-1-6667-4472-9
ISBN: 978-1-6667-4473-6

09/16/22

Scripture quotations are taken from the New Revised Standard Version Bible (NRSV), copyright 1989 by National Council of the Churches of Christ in the United States of America. Used by permission. All rights reserved.

Contents

Preface | vii
Abbreviations | xi

1 A Life Mired in Conflict | 1
2 An Anatomist Confronts Ethics | 21
3 A Scientist's View of a Pandemic | 40
4 Vaccines, Vaccine Mandates, Freedom, and Love of Neighbor | 58
5 Cystic Fibrosis: Looking to Science for Hope | 76
6 The Embryo, the Reproductive Technologies, and Christian Faithfulness | 95
7 Biomedical Technology, Christian Thinking, and the Public Square | 114
8 Gender Issues: Same-Sex Attraction | 133
9 Anatomy of an Academic Life | 153

Glossary | 169
Bibliography | 173
General Index | 179
Scripture Index | 183

Preface

IT IS A TRUISM that as one gets older one tends to look back and assess what it is you have or have not accomplished. You are also strikingly aware of how things have changed, whether standards, expectations, or dominant thought-forms. As a biomedical scientist, changes have been the norm over the years I have been involved and have commented on the challenges presented to Christians and the Christian faith. By the same token, Christian responses have also changed, since what is regarded as acceptable or unacceptable to many Christians today has also changed. Consequently, most biomedical debates in the 1970s or 1980s are almost unrecognizable today. This can be disconcerting to anyone wanting to come to terms with the legitimacy or otherwise of the arguments at the heart of these debates and wanting some assurance about the most appropriate stance to take on these highly practical matters that frequently have deeply personal (and faith) overtones.

Is it ethical for a pregnant woman to undergo prenatal diagnostic tests to find out whether the developing fetus has a suspected congenital genetic or chromosomal abnormality? Under what circumstances, if ever, is it ethical for a Christian believer to undergo an abortion? Is it ever legitimate for an individual to undergo hormonal and surgical procedures to change their gender? Under what circumstances might an individual agree to have a brain implant, knowing this could have repercussions for their personal identity? Are there Christian reasons for refusing to be vaccinated against COVID-19, or any other virus, for that matter? The questions are

Preface

endless, or so it seems, and they are questions that our forebears did not have to face. They are scientific and clinical questions, but they are also theological ones, since they strike at the heart of what it means to act as a Christian (or equally as a religious believer of another tradition). We are all involved, as patients, parents, family members, friends, members of the society in which we live, or health professionals. None can completely escape the many tentacles of biomedical technology, both for good and for ill. Neither can we escape the many controversies that are integral to our responses, both within the church and beyond its walls in the society in which churches are embedded.

I write as someone trained as a medical doctor, human anatomist, and neuroscientist, with what I like to describe as a considerable interest in ethical issues related to the human body. I am, therefore, very much a practicing scientist. However, I am also a practicing Christian, who seeks guidance from the Christian Scriptures. Over the years I have moved increasingly into bioethics, although I have deliberately limited my interests to bioethical issues related to the human body and human tissue and in particular to the dead human body. However, even as my interests in bioethics have come increasingly to the fore, I have never ceased to be a scientist with the interests and drives of a scientist. Neither have I ceased to be an academic and researcher who is driven by the challenges of ongoing scientific developments. In the biomedical arena these have continued to be vigorous and enticing. On many occasions I have wished I could close the door on my many interests and put them behind me. But this has not been possible for two reasons: the developments themselves are inherently fascinating, and they pose ongoing challenges for people of faith.

My commitment to academic exploration has had two consequences. In the first place, I have written extensively for academic audiences via peer-reviewed books, book chapters, and journal articles. These have principally been directed at general academic audiences rather than Christian ones. The second is that my specialism has mainly been governed by my profession, that is, anatomy, and within anatomy the importance we place on the dignity of the dead human body. This has led to advocacy for the use of bodies bequeathed to anatomy departments for dissection and research as opposed to the use of unclaimed bodies. While these interests have not been specifically Christian ones, and are not usually of much interest to Christian writers and audiences, they reflect values dear to Christians, aimed as they are at enhancing the centrality of human welfare and human dignity.

Preface

My specifically Christian writings have largely, but not entirely, been on beginning-of-life issues, calling on my knowledge of embryology and the early stages of human development. However, it has become progressively more evident that advances in medical technology have had significant repercussions for everyone and certainly not just for Christians.[1] This is because we have become increasingly dependent upon technological interventions at all stages of our lives. As embodied creatures, these interventions have changed our expectations of how we live, what we expect out of life, and even of the extent to which we depend upon God (and whether science is of any relevance here). It is these theological repercussions that I have attempted to confront in my more recent writings. These have included the extent to which we design babies, the increasing challenges posed by an understanding of stem cells and their potential, the ever-burgeoning insights provided by neuroscience, and a possible future world populated by clones and cyborgs. In the midst of this ever-changing world, Christians, like others, are confronted by the increasing powers made available by genetic advances, the intrusion of brain modification procedures in therapy and possibly as a way of actually improving human experiences, the scenarios opened up by technological enhancements of morality, and profound queries about whether aging is inevitable or is a disease to be eliminated.[2]

My intention in the present book is not to retrace these debates or cover all of them, although inevitably some will feature. They will reflect some of the more recent debates in which I have been involved, all of which have a bearing on the close relationship between my faith and my science, or more broadly faith and science. A major contrast from previous writings is the more personal tenor of my writing in this instance. I will reveal far more of where I am coming from as a Christian, why I am a Christian, and particularly how my Christianity and my science interact. In doing this I shall call on themes that have characterized my writings in the anatomical area. As a human anatomist I have dealt with the human body in its many facets, both in life and in death, although most of my efforts have been

---

1. Thoughts along these lines were brought together in my 2013 book: *The Peril and Promise of Medical Technology*.

2. Some of my writings on these and related topics are to be found in the following books: *Valuing People: Human Value in a World of Medical Technology*, 1999; *Clones: The Clowns of Technology?* 2001; *Designers of the Future: Who Makes the Decisions?* 2005; *Bioethics: When the Challenges of Life Become too Difficult*, 2005; edited with John Elford, *A Tangled Web: Medicine and Theology in Dialogue*, 2009; edited with John Elford, *A Glass Darkly: Medicine and Theology in Further Dialogue*, 2010.

Preface

directed at the latter—the body in death. This should come as no surprise to Christians, since we are embodied beings, who live with particular bodies with certain flaws, no matter what the origin of those flaws, and no matter what ways there may or may not be of alleviating them. As an anatomist and a scientist, I reflect on these matters every day, with their vast panoply of ethical dimensions, conflicts, and mysteries.

My hope is that I am able to use the fruits of my thinking and understanding, no matter how limited some of them undoubtedly are, to throw light on profound dilemmas. This is no easy task, but I also hope it will demonstrate how a Christian and scientist approaches issues confronting every one of us. These reflections have enabled me to bring together these various strands in my thinking, strands that have gradually emerged over many years of writing and teaching. Most of the work has been undertaken in a public university in which I have sought to function as an active academic in my chosen professional area.

A word on referencing. Since this is not an academic monograph, I have made no attempt to provide detailed references or notes. A limited number of relevant ones are included, but these are not intended to be extensive. However, when putting together the bibliography, I was very surprised at how much literature I had used, and also at the many fields that have been covered. That was never my intention, but it serves to show the breadth of my interests that have on occasion proved difficult to control.

As always, I would like to acknowledge and thank Beryl, my wife, for her immense forbearance, as I have ruminated and tossed ideas over in my brain (or mind if you like), lost in my own thoughts. I would also like to thank those who have partnered with me in some of my writings over the years and have been prepared to enter forbidding terrain. Their names appear repeatedly in the bibliography! And, of course, there are those who have been prepared to publish my writings, especially when they have stepped outside well-trodden territory and have crossed disciplinary boundaries. To these and many others, *diolch yn fawr*.

Dunedin, July 2022

Abbreviations

ACART	Advisory Committee on Assisted Reproductive Technology
ARTs	artificial reproductive technologies
CF	cystic fibrosis
CFTR	cystic fibrosis transmembrane regulator
CMDA	Christian Medical and Dental Associations
COVID	coronavirus disease
CRISPR	clustered regularly interspaced short palindromic repeats
DNA	deoxyribonucleic acid
ESCs	embryonic stem cells
FASD	fetal alcohol spectrum disorder
HEK	human embryonic kidney [cell line]
ICSI	intracytoplasmic sperm injection
IVF	*in vitro* fertilization
ICM	inner cell mass
IPSCs	induced pluripotent stem cells
LGBTQI	lesbian, gay, bisexual, transgender, queer, intersexed

Abbreviations

MMR	measles, mumps, rubella [vaccine]
NIH	National Institutes of Health
NIPT	non-invasive prenatal testing
OSA	opposite-sex attracted
PGD	preimplantation genetic diagnosis
SARS-CoV-2	severe acute respiratory syndrome coronavirus 2
SCNT	somatic cell nuclear transfer
SSA	same-sex attracted
UCL	University College London

1

A Life Mired in Conflict

Unexpected Directions

LIFE CAN TAKE UNEXPECTED turns. I could not possibly have imagined when I set out as a medical student in 1958 that I would end up as an anatomist, and in particular a neuroscientist, and one with a profound interest in both ethical and administrative issues. Neither could I have contemplated that my thinking would be undertaken within a predominantly Christian context. In 1965, even as I started out on an academic career in the anatomy department at University College London, I still could not have envisaged that it would take me along such apparently circuitous paths. On the surface it may look as though not too much has changed, apart from changing universities and countries. After all, I am still in an anatomy department, and for many years neuroscience constituted the dominant part of my academic life; it was only after a number of years that bioethics gradually emerged and became integral to my academic endeavors. Alongside these developments was an additional one, and this was an interest in, and commitment to, a wide range of administrative undertakings. Throughout all these changes and transitions, I have sought to be guided by my Christian faith. I have never left behind my allegiance to science and the scientific method, nor to the commitment that, when used wisely and with discernment, this is an important means by which God blesses human beings. For me, the broad framework within which I have functioned has been that of a robust and well-grounded Christian faith.

At the Margins

My digressions into bioethics have never deviated from this fundamental stance. I have never become a professional (fully paid-up) bioethicist, but, as I have always phrased it, I am a scientist (more specifically, anatomist) with a serious interest in applied ethics. It was this that led me into the emerging field of anatomy and ethics. At heart I am a scientist committed to the rigors of scientific analysis. The same applies to my thinking as a Christian. I have never sought to leave my science behind, an attitude that helps explain my unease whenever I encounter theologians (and bioethicists) who seek to address questions around early human development, or a viral pandemic, with practically no reference to any scientific input. For me this amounts to a denial of the whole scientific enterprise and of all the good things that God has bestowed upon his creation through the human creativity underlying science and, in my case, biomedical science. Only in this way do we get a full-orbed glimpse into God's wonderful world.

Neither could I have envisaged that these approaches would lead me into a world of unease and tension, on occasion in the academic world but more frequently in the Christian world. It is as if much that I have thought about and written about has been at fault lines, akin to geological fault lines, where there is always some movement but from time to time much more dramatic shifts of the tectonic plates as one plate rubs over another to cause a substantial eruption at the surface. The biomedical world is replete with developments that for some are disturbing and for others exciting but generally a mixture of the two. How else can one describe the furor in the reproductive area, whether it be the emergence and blossoming of *in vitro* fertilization (IVF) to CRISPR gene editing, or the production of artificial human embryos (iBlastoids) without resorting to the fertilization normally dependent upon eggs and sperm all the way to the production of human-monkey chimeras? Some days it seems the possibilities and ingenuity of scientists are endless, but with endless possibilities come equally endless ethical and, for Christians, theological quandaries.

To make matters more demanding, the immediate responses to most of these developments are either alarmist and negative or unduly positive. Neither is helpful for serious ongoing debate, but all too readily simplistic solutions or responses dominate. My role, as I have seen it, is to bring a Christian perspective to these fast-moving debates, taking seriously the science and its potential contributions to human health and the welfare of a broad swathe of people but always aware of the overconfidence of some scientists.

A Life Mired in Conflict

My Faith Journeys

My journey as a Christian began during my teens, as I struggled with religious questions and where they fitted alongside my growing awareness of evolutionary humanism and how it sought to make sense of humans within a vast, evolving universe. A dominant attraction for me at that stage was evolutionary thinking and evolutionary humanism, as in the writings of Julian Huxley, who even advocated a "religion without revelation." I did not see any great conflict here, because I found these writings attractive and stimulating. What was of lasting relevance for me was the pull of broad evolutionary thinking trying to make sense of the world, the centrality of science and especially of human science, and religion. I found all in their different ways enticing and informative. I was not in a position to delve into any of them in great detail, but that was not of paramount importance for me at that stage of my thinking. Little did I know how significant each of these was to be as my life course developed and took form over the coming years.

My upbringing in a traditional non-conformist Protestant church had in no way prepared me for what I was to later regard as truly Christian thinking. I had not been brought face-to-face with the good news of Jesus Christ. I had heard about the importance of being concerned about the state of society, and there is no doubt this stemmed from Christian concerns. This was an expression of social Christianity, and one can sympathize with why this was so emphasized in urban South Wales, with its poverty, drudgery, ill health, and unrelenting work in coal mines and steel works. But there was no confrontation with the person and work of Christ in salvation.

I was searching for an elusive something, since I was well aware that my religiosity was not the answer. That finally came from biblical preachers in the Pentecostal and Evangelical traditions, through which I was learning more about the gospel and its Christ-centered message. Each year brought me closer to Christ as I read and thought more and more about Christianity from numerous, often conflicting, sources. Things were falling into place, and I was becoming increasingly knowledgeable about the gospel and convinced about its significance for me. I was also beginning to think about how the sort of Christianity I was being introduced to would fit in with my interest in evolutionary biology and anthropology. Everything eventually fell into place a month before I left the Welsh valleys for medical school in London, and the stimulus came from the New Testament and the apostle Paul's Letter to the Romans (Rom 10:1–4):

> Brothers and sisters, my heart's desire and prayer to God for them is that they may be saved. I can testify that they have a zeal for God, but it is not enlightened. For, being ignorant of the righteousness that comes from God, and seeking to establish their own, they have not submitted to God's righteousness. For Christ is the end of the law so that there may be righteousness for everyone who believes.

This spoke directly to me; this was precisely where I was at. I had been trying for the previous few years to be zealous for God, to earn my salvation, and now I realized that there was only one answer, and that lay outside myself. It was to be found in God's initiative and in Jesus Christ and in him alone. There was no need to argue one's way into the kingdom of God or to prove that he was the creator of all things. He alone was the key to salvation. My life had been set on a new trajectory.

It is probably true to say that my conversion had a powerful intellectual core. It had taken place gradually over three years or so, and the elements had been slowly falling into place. While I am unable to put my finger on all the constituent parts, I had looked closely at a host of Christian beliefs alongside my ongoing fascination with evolutionary humanism. For me, some of the grand vistas of scientific thinking were far more compelling than what I had known of Christianity previously. However, an encounter with Jesus Christ was vastly different, and, as I came to appreciate in the years ahead, it was to prove intensely satisfying intellectually. But one thing was clear to me even at that time, and this was that I had no interest in a faith characterized by simplistic answers and a restricted view of the world and reality. I wanted an exciting vista, one that took serious note of the big questions raised by the world I was encountering.

Consequently, I have always placed major store by the centrality of the "mind" for the Christian faith, not some arid intellectualistic faith but one that consistently seeks understanding at all levels. I have never been attracted to an emotionally-driven faith, even as I concede the importance of the Christian faith for our emotions, our longings, and our strivings. The faith, after all, has implications for every facet of our beings. Nevertheless, for me the cognitive element is a crucial element I have never wished to downplay. I return to this in chapter 9.

The date of my religious awakening was well-timed, as it was just a month before I exited the Welsh valleys for University College London (UCL). I had little idea what lay ahead, nor did I have any insights into the caliber or character of the medical school that I was entering. Only later did I realize the significance of a medical school that was an integral part of a leading university that extended far beyond the confines of medicine and science. I may have spent too much time trawling around the stacks of the main library, but for me they represented a door into a fascinating, intriguing world, especially with their insights into the history of medicine and science. Against this backdrop, two influences in London stand out as crucial for my future development. The contrast between them is remarkable: a scientific humanist and an evangelical non-conformist preacher.

The scientific humanist was J. Z. Young (1907–97), head of the anatomy department at UCL. He was a zoologist and comparative anatomist, not a human anatomist, and was probably one of the foremost invertebrate anatomists of the century. He was one of the people who taught me to think, and a highlight of my time in anatomy were the one-to-one tutorials I had with him during my honors year in anatomy. It was the comments he made on my essays that were so penetrating and educational. I lapped up his book *Doubt and Certainty in Science* (1950) and the later *Philosophy and the Brain* (1982). During our preclinical medical course, he gave a weekly lecture on aspects of human biology, such as population numbers and evolution, and later published them as *An Introduction to the Study of Man*. I was engrossed, even if the clinically-minded were less so.

In religious terms, J. Z. was a leading scientific humanist in Britain, and yet it was he from whom I gained a huge amount of insight that was of inestimable value for my thinking and analyzing ideas and concepts. Years later, as I have looked back on this, it demonstrated to me that it is possible to learn from those with quite different philosophies and perspectives from your own. To restrict yourself to those with identical horizons to your own is to erect a fence around your world, and for me that has always been self-defeating and limiting.

A counterpoint to J. Z. Young was provided by Martyn Lloyd-Jones (1899–1981), the other seminal influence on my thinking. It would be difficult to get two more contrasting figures. Martyn Lloyd-Jones, widely referred to as "the Doctor," was minister of Westminster Chapel London. When I attended this church in the late 1950s and early 1960s, he was at his height as a preacher and biblical expositor, an intellectual of no mean stature. And so, while I have commented on the contrast, there was this similarity—they were both intellectual giants. And for me this was life-changing. In their different ways both taught me to think and analyze.

I lapped up the theology and the thinking, as my mind was stretched by the Doctor's detailed analysis of Paul's Letter to the Ephesians and a series of lectures on revivals. I can well remember Sunday evening evangelistic sermons on the later chapters in the Gospel of Matthew as he spoke about "man," meaning human beings and their future. I was entranced. I had never heard anything like this before. This was an influence that has never left me, no matter how much I may subsequently have queried some aspects of "Reformed" theology as expressed in their twentieth- and twenty-first-century guises. It laid the foundations for my theological thinking and set me on the path of always doing my best as a non-theologian to apply theological thinking to all the applied issues to which I have given attention over the years. Unfortunately, perhaps, it has made me critical of papers delivered in science-faith conferences that provide good analyses of the science but fail to engage seriously with relevant Christian perspectives.

It was during these years that I started thinking seriously about going into scientific research rather than into clinical medicine. There were many reasons for this change of direction, and some Christians around me expressed the view that this was not the direction a young Christian should take. The reason: I would lose my faith. While listening respectfully to these dire warnings, I ventured on. My faith in God was too strong and too well thought through to be deterred by what I interpreted as well-meaning detractions.

I have always regarded myself as a biblically-based Christian in the sense that I have sought to be guided and directed by biblical precepts and applied principles emerging from these. I abhor being known by any label, since labels can be used to bring debate to an end and categorize people into alien categories. I have benefited from a wide range of theological writers, including those with perspectives quite different from my own, especially on ethical questions. In short, I have felt that I have benefited from a wide a circle of people of faith and of no faith. I have never wanted to limit the scope of insights available to me.

My worldview stems from the Reformation and its many heirs. While the dominant theologians have varied in their emphases, there are clear threads running through their stances, threads that have had a profound influence on my own thinking. No matter what the differences between many of these, they have been one in what have come to be regarded as the four characteristics of the evangelical expression of the Christian faith, the so-called Bebbington quadrilateral: ultimate authority lies in Scripture; emphasis on the atonement based in Christ's crucifixion; the centrality of the conversion experience; the gospel has implications for how we live in this world.[1]

These headings do not provide all the answers to any of our contemporary issues, but they are the ingredients from which I have never wished to depart. They constitute the essential thrust of my faith and of my way of thinking. They serve as the departure point for my analyses of, and attitudes towards, most topics, and to which I have sought to cling throughout what have frequently been turbulent waters. They provide the basis of a robust form of Christianity, a faith that is not for the faint-hearted. I have never had the slightest temptation to become a fundamentalist or literalist. This was not my background, and my thinking has always been far broader than this. I simply do not function in this way; it is alien to my DNA.[2]

Moving between Science and Faith

Throughout, I have sought to stress two prevailing drivers in my life: my faith and my vocation, or more specifically my faith as a biblically-based Christian and my training as a biomedical scientist. I find it impossible to separate the two, since each influences and informs the other. I have often had occasion to reflect on how different I would have been had I been trained as a theologian rather than as a scientist, or alternatively as a scientist with a secular worldview. While I cannot vouch for the accuracy of any predictions, there is no doubt that, on both counts, I would have approached applied ethical questions rather differently. I have never wanted to divide my life into distinct spiritual and secular compartments. I have wanted my life to stand as a Christ-centered one, where Christ is as relevant in my thinking about scientific and ethical matters as about church-related matters. On most occasions within the academic sphere (as within any professional area) this is not made explicit, but the values I espouse and the hopes I cling onto are, I trust, ones emanating from the Christ revealed

---

1. Bebbington, *Evangelicalism in Modern Britain*.

2. I have stated my concern with being labelled and placed in any easy-to-define category, although I accept that, theologically, I fit within the broad compass of Evangelicalism. However, the vituperative recent debates over what constitutes Evangelicalism as a movement, the ways in which this designation is employed in different countries, and the condemnation that has come my way from elements within Evangelicalism, make me wary of wishing to be known primarily as an Evangelical. It is for this reason that I frequently describe my stance as that of a biblically-based Christian, or as a theologically conservative Christian.

in Scripture. It also means I am committed to the view that science can, in some instances, help us come to grips with the Bible and its interpretation.

I want people to think and be challenged so that they can work through their own responses to difficult problems. I have never viewed it as my role to provide them with ready-made answers or with dogmatic stances in murky ethical waters. For those who are not Christians, my aim is to sketch paths that are reasonable and that take the evidence seriously. I want those of faith to take the Bible seriously, and to use it to inform their thinking on very difficult and complex issues. Although the Bible does not provide detailed answers in many of the areas with which I deal, it has exceedingly helpful insights for those who seek to follow Jesus. Accepting that there will not be categorical answers to highly complex contemporary issues within the pages of the Bible, I have no doubt it contains helpful ways forward that will provide a context for responsible decision-making.

I am grateful for what science has to offer. I am also deeply conscious of the subtle temptations created by excessive dependence upon a scientific approach to reality, including the allures of technology. I reject any scientistic answers where science becomes the be-all-and-end-all of existence; that is to make it an idol, with quasi-god-like attributes.[3] This is far removed from my stance that we should view Scripture and science as two sides of the same coin, where each has its own special contribution to make to a holistic view of God's world. Each also operates within its own framework, and, for me, the respective frameworks are to be taken seriously and adhered to as far as possible.

Two passages of Scripture come repeatedly to mind as relevant to my dual quest. When children were brought to Jesus, not only did he welcome them, but he also used the occasion to shine light onto a basic truth about attitude: "Anyone who does not receive the kingdom of God as a little child will never enter it" (Luke 18:17). Openness, honesty, truthfulness, and uncomplicated inquisitiveness are basic prerequisites for the life of faith. There has to be a desire to learn new truths and walk in new ways. There is yet much to be revealed if only we will listen and respond. Interestingly, very similar requirements are placed on us by science as we respond to new evidence and new insights.

The other passage comes from Paul's first Letter to the Corinthian church, with its insistence on the pre-eminence of love over even such crucial attitudes as faith and hope. In working this out Paul reminds his readers

3. Hutchinson, *Can a Scientist Believe in Miracles?*

that, at present, our understanding and knowledge are partial. "For now we see in a mirror, dimly, but then we will see face-to-face. Now I know only in part; then I will know fully, even as I have been fully known" (1 Cor 13:12). In other words, what we see now is a poor reflection of reality. No matter how it is phrased, even our most magnificent and compelling explanations and insights are, in the final analysis, limited and in time will be revealed as inadequate or at the very least in need of improvement. And this applies to both science and theology. This is a salutary thought for any of us, especially those engaged in cutting-edge academic endeavors. It is more obvious in the sciences, where the life cycle of concepts may be a matter of months or a few years at the most. This does not invalidate the earlier work, but it demonstrates all too clearly the transitoriness of so much we spend so much effort on. Ideas in theology may appear more steadfast, and yet there are cycles of interpretation, so that what was *avant garde* in the early 1900s is of little more than historic curiosity a century later.

Humility, and an awareness of our far-from-assured grasp of what may appear to be assured knowledge, are basic prerequisites in science and theology. We are limited human beings, and our limitations should keep us from pontificating in both areas. This should set the scene for rich dialogue with others, a willingness to learn from others, and hopefully to share perspectives with others. The fact that life is rarely like this, and that we erect rigid walls to shield us from outside influences, is testimony to our defensiveness and unwillingness to be open to others, even those ostensibly who have much in common with us.

One characteristic that scientists bring to the science-faith area is their discomfort with less-than-precise thinking and their lack of patience with vagueness. This may be why their writing tends to be much sparser than that of those in the humanities. Ideally, they formulate hypotheses or ideas which they then set about testing and disproving. While it would be unrealistic to think that scientists act like this in every area of their lives, if they are consistent in their thinking, they will tend to be logical and precise. This is a far cry from the grand conceptualizing of theology, as it deals with vast questions of meaning and God's kingdom. I have attempted to straddle both spheres, realizing that this is a balancing act I have not always mastered and being acutely aware that I have failed on more than one occasion to achieve what I set out to achieve or that I have been misunderstood.

At the Margins

Where Does Bioethics Fit In?

A constant feature of the science-faith debate is that it has excluded bioethics, since this is generally placed in a category of its own as though it has nothing to do with science. Increasingly, this has struck me as a strange anomaly. Bioethics deals with ethical issues raised by current developments brought about by explorations in the biomedical world. This is cutting-edge science, nothing more and nothing less. There is no doubt it raises numerous queries for the Christian faith, as well as for other expressions of religious faith. Where is God in gene technology? Should technology such as this be used to alleviate congenital aberrations? Is this going too far and intruding as an unwelcome guest into a God-ordained sacred space? The questions are endless, all of which are relevant for those of faith, even if some are more useful than others.[4] Nevertheless, there are differences in the character of the questions and the answers we seek. This is because the generalities that frequently dominate traditional science-faith dialogue are replaced by specific queries. Can we proceed in this or that direction? Can the use of this procedure be justified? Are we pushing our technological abilities too far? Is moving in this direction in the patient's interests or not? These ethical questions would never have surfaced were it not for the science underlying them. And these ethical questions are frequently of direct relevance to one's faith and worldview as well as one's health and wellbeing.

Biomedical endeavors are inseparable from specifics demanding precise answers and directives. Seeing God in medicine or healing is ambiguous, since we think we have been let down when healing does not come, when there is no cure, and when the patient or our loved one dies. When faced by dilemmas like these, we are brought face-to-face with a suffering God rather than a triumphant God. If confronted by inevitable decline, where is God? Can science help more than prayer, or are both letting us down? There is no escape from the interplay between God and science, often at a deeply personal level. This is where the "bio" of bioethics reminds us that this is not abstract theorizing but real life with real consequences at every level of what we are as human beings.

The challenge for Christians is neither to decry nor eulogize technological advances but to seek to put them in perspective. A Christian paradigm faces up to the inevitability of suffering and mortality not in a fatalistic

---

4. Sections of this chapter are based on my writings in "The Changing Face of the Science-Faith Dialogue in a Biomedical Arena."

way, but by seeking to be faithful to Christ in the midst of suffering. When confronted by suffering and uncertainty, the Christian is to examine the technology available and the manner in which it might be used to assist in this situation. What will bring glory to God? How best can I respond as a follower of Christ? This is as much a science-faith duopoly as is anything in the physical sciences.

Technology is a tool to be employed in the service of Christ. For medical scientists this is encouragement to excel at research both fundamental and applied. Scientists are cooperating with God in understanding his creation as they strive to uncover more of the wonder and intricacy of the human body along with its complexity and regenerative powers. In helping to conquer and quell the ravages of disease, they are bringing control and order to that which is disordered and destructive. In helping to increase life expectancy and the quality of that life, they are giving opportunities to those who would otherwise lack them, especially to those in the majority world where life expectancy remains low. For those of faith in those societies, they are being enabled to appreciate God far better and to worship him all the better. In principle, scientists are helping to enhance the beauty of human life and the depth of human community. In this way they are providing a means by which people can experience a far richer quality of life, both individually and in community. By the same token there are limits to these endeavors, because extending life for its own sake and inflicting onerous burdens upon, say, aging patients can detract from the good and the worthy. Wisdom and discernment are central to any Christian assessment of how technology should be employed.

The biomedical area is ripe for investigation as an integral feature of the science (technology)-faith domain. We are diminished to the extent that we relegate it to a category of its own in which science is seen to play a negligible role. Those scientists who are Christians are to be encouraged to take an active part in this world and to devote their energies to increasing our understanding of the body in its many dimensions and in alleviating suffering and loss on the part of humans like ourselves. The realization that we are living in an imperfect world with its "not yet" character should constrain our pretensions and idealism, but neither does it militate against the contribution that scientists make to better the world and human beings within it.

A constant temptation for everyone is to think we have the answer—the correct answer and possibly the only acceptable answer. And yet there is much we do not know, and there will be doubts. Whether in science or in theology (or in philosophy or economics for that matter), our understanding is always incomplete, or our interpretation may be flawed. We may be wrong. None of this is a challenge to our faith or to the reliability of much in science. There are clear signposts in both domains, but so often those signposts do not provide infallible guidance. There is no escape from the particular cultural context within which we live and function, including the time in history where we find ourselves. And as individuals we have our own histories, our own limitations, our own prejudices.

Human beings are not all-knowing, no matter how able they (we) are. As images of God, humans are privileged creatures, but they constantly fall short and will continue to do so this side of the eschaton. The academic life as researcher and scholar has taught me humility and a profound knowledge of both the temporary nature of all knowledge and the fallibility of all judgments, including my own. But it has also shown me the vast opportunities it opens up, and for this I am deeply grateful.

Over a number of years, I have become close to a couple of theological ethicists whose theological positions have been different from mine. However, our ethical contributions have complemented each other in many positive ways, and in both cases, we have undertaken joint writing projects. I have benefited enormously from both, since they have each proved to be a breath of fresh air; we have thought deeply about topics of mutual interest and have discovered a respect for each other's contributions. The main components appeared to be a willingness to look afresh at social and ethical issues and, when necessary, a preparedness to change position, to admit the relevance of new knowledge and new insights, along with being willing to admit that our individual responses may be wrong. Underlying these characteristics is the need for a high degree of realism about the science on the one hand, and the central features of a Christian response on the other. Together they constitute a dynamic matrix with a considerable degree of give and take. After all I do not know everything and I am certainly not omnicompetent, recognition of which demands humility. But, some may say, this is the path to haziness and fuzziness, and a willingness to accept all the latest fads and trends. I disagree, because in my estimation, readiness to change one's position on some matters at the science-ethics border need not signify any relinquishing of fundamental beliefs and stances.

A Life Mired in Conflict

Finding Myself the Object of Controversy

The science-faith area can give the impression of having all the hallmarks of a fusty academic domain inhabited by erudite types more at home in libraries lined by prestigious-looking tomes and isolated from the real world. Whatever truth there may, on occasion, be in that description, it is far removed from the multiplicity of dilemmas created by current biomedical research and debate. The demands made upon anyone seeking to address them are considerable, and these are accentuated by those working from a Christian base. Unfortunately, the result may be open conflict, far removed from the cozy halls of measured academic debate. I shall return to reasons why this may be the case, but before I do, I shall recount an event that had far-reaching repercussions for my life at the science-faith intersection.

This happened totally unexpectedly in 1984. Prior to this event it had never occurred to me that I would ever be regarded as an object of dissension. After all, I was an academic working quietly as a relatively anonymous academic in a university—a true ivory tower in a small island country at the edge of the known world. I had no political pretensions and no stake in promulgating any ethical or theological cause. But somehow some saw me as a threat to the health of the Christian church in the United States.[5]

From anonymity I was thrust into the limelight as an arch proponent of abortion on demand, and in doing this had set out to promote the most liberal form of abortion imaginable. This was news to me, but I had no say in the manner in which I was depicted by certain Christians, intent on exposing me as an arch opponent of all that was good and true. And the cause of this mayhem? It was my book *Brave New People*[6] that had been very severely criticized by an anonymous writer, and following this letters were also arriving at the offices of the publisher, InterVarsity Press (IVP), objecting to its publication, a move advocated by a pro-life advocacy group.

The publisher's offices were picketed. There was a flow of critical letters advocating that people discontinue their financial support of Intervarsity Christian Fellowship and that booksellers boycott all IVP publications. In spite of the support of a number of prominent theologians and ethicists, the

---

5. The events referred to in this section are outlined in more detail in my book: *Coping with Controversy*, 1996.

6. This was published in both the United Kingdom and the United States by the respective IVP publishers. There was no furor in the United Kingdom, where it had originally been published, and where great care had been taken to avoid any unnecessary controversy. Compare the 1984 IVP edition and the 1985 Eerdmans edition.

book was withdrawn from the American market, although it was shortly brought out by another publisher (Eerdmans).

This was the first occasion in the then forty-three-year history of IVP that a book of theirs had been withdrawn from circulation.[7] My reason for writing had been to inform Christians and others about the major technological developments in reproductive biology that was in its infancy in 1984. My focus of attention, therefore, was *in vitro* fertilization (IVF), artificial insemination, cloning, amniocentesis, genetic counselling, and the whole technological environment responsible for these developments. I had also attempted to view these procedures within a biblical and Christian framework.

The furor, however, was not over my treatment of these issues. My crime, if that is not too strong a word, lay in the chapter on therapeutic abortion, where I had apparently transgressed all the principles of Evangelicalism by allowing for abortion under a very limited number of circumstances. Completely unawares, and certainly against my own desires, I found myself cast as a leader of the pro-abortion forces within Evangelicalism. No justification was required to support this assignation in spite of the fact that *Brave New People* only incidentally dealt with therapeutic abortion and hardly touched on abortion in general terms. I found that my "heretical" views had earned me notoriety within certain American evangelical circles. In the eyes of some, my views were so dangerous that they had to be censored. That censorship was duly carried out by a few self-appointed guardians of evangelical morality, who conducted a vociferous and concerted campaign against the book, myself, and the publishers.

This incident occurred almost forty years ago and is historical. Why then do I raise it? For a number of reasons. It demonstrates in unequivocal terms the extremely fine line that anyone writing from a conservative Christian perspective has to tread. Once you move outside publishing solely in academic journals or with academic presses, you are exposed to the full force of some who think they know the path you should tread and will do their best to prevent you expressing any alternative viewpoint. In spite of such problems, I have no doubt there is a valid role for scientists to speak into highly contested territory, since in their absence the science-faith debate will be a much impoverished one. It will also amount to a denial that God can be glorified through the works of his hands and through the work of those in a position to unpack the intricacies of his creation. It is also important to hold fast to the crucial place of truth in contemporary debate and

---

7. This is explained in Le Peau and Doll, *Heart. Soul. Mind. Strength*, 89–94.

on the importance of depicting fairly the views of those holding alternative viewpoints to one's own and possibly to the generally accepted position.

The significance of being truthful and dealing as honestly as possible with the evidence has come to the fore much more recently in both political and Christian circles in relation to COVID vaccines and vaccine mandates (see chapter 4). The emergence of so-called fake news and the blatant twisting of facts have seriously disrupted meaningful and productive discussions across the science-faith borders. Tragically, this has occurred in some conservative Christian circles, to the detriment of serious debate.

Dissecting How We Navigate Science-Faith Debates

Bioethical debate is strewn with arguments that stem from "one-issue advocacy." The plethora of issues that could be raised become concentrated into just one: "Agreement is required on issue X." Issues A–H are ignored; all that matters is this one issue. Anyone who does not agree on this particular issue is not regarded as "one of us," no matter what else is agreed upon; issue X has been elevated to the one cardinal issue, it has been elevated to the top of a crucial hierarchy. Or, to use different terminology, it has become the litmus test for faithfulness to our group, no matter which group that may be. While approaches of this nature can arise in any sphere, today they emerge repeatedly in religious spheres, particularly in more conservative ones.

I have encountered this problem in the biomedical sciences and predominantly in the embryological and reproductive areas. This is usually expressed by revulsion at abortion and at the unjustified deaths of countless numbers of "unborn children." I have considerable sympathy with this response in general ethical and theological terms, since I do not consider that any prenatal life should be carelessly destroyed. And yet I have concerns that an unyielding opposition to abortion under all circumstances can have unforeseen consequences, especially when interpreted as protecting all prenatal human life, from "conception" onwards. The protection of the fetus (eight weeks gestation onwards) has been translated into protection of the embryo (fertilization to eight weeks gestation). With this move the discussion takes on new dimensions, as it has been relocated out of pastoral ethical territory into the biomedical research domain, simply because this is where research on early human development takes place.

The anti-abortion/pro-life stance that had as its primary goal the protection of fetuses in danger of being discarded by their mothers has now been widened substantially to oppose the destruction of all embryos from their point of origin in the laboratory. Consequently, a clinical ethical debate has been transmuted into a research ethics debate, and the inviolability of fetuses has been extended to cover the inviolability of embryos and blastocysts (very early embryos at five to nine days of development). It is at this juncture that the science-faith debate rears its head. Abortion is not a highly technological activity; it is the province of the clinician. The faith issues implicit within the rightness and wrongness of abortion in general, and of any individual abortion, do not involve ground-breaking science as such.

The same cannot be said for clinical procedures or research that manipulates embryos in the laboratory (*in vitro* procedures), from IVF and preimplantation genetic diagnosis (PGD) to research using viable human embryos. Here scientific investigations are to the fore, and any constraints imposed upon these activities on the basis of religious objections are very much science-faith territory. Commonly encountered pro-life positions oppose any such uses of human embryos on the ground that they destroy human life with a moral value equal to that of all born (postnatal) human beings. Human life is claimed to be sacred, the sanctity of which extends from the very earliest indications of existence. This raises the specter of needing to protect the interests of the embryo to the exclusion of all other competing ethical, social, and personal concerns (see chapter 6). Once this stance is accepted as the only legitimate position for biblically-based Christians, dialogue becomes unsustainable.

As a biomedical scientist, this approach represents foreign territory. Ethical debate in general, let alone within a Christian context, does not lend itself to polarization of this nature. There are always numerous competing factors to be taken into account, and frequently these point in different directions. For Christians, the bottom line should be the scriptural and theological justification for such extensive protection, extending from every embryo ever brought into existence to every pregnancy regardless of the personal, cultural, and health context within which it takes place. Comments of this nature are not intended to justify liberal ethical perspectives, but they are a call for precision in ethical determinations. In the absence of the latter, science-faith debates will be nothing other than fraught.

Any suggestion that a particular Christian viewpoint is indubitably right and all others are inevitably wrong in debates traversing a multitude of disciplinary and philosophical outlooks will end in unproductive conflict. Jesus had a great deal to say about the folly of judging others and of setting ourselves up as authorities (Matt 7:1–5). It is all too easy to condemn some minor deviation from what you consider the truth and ignore a far more serious inconsistency in your own stance. Under these circumstances, it becomes very difficult to learn from others, particularly those with scientific insights as well as those fellow believers with different perspectives from one's own.

The abortion debate highlights what I see as the contrast between idealism and realism, between those who are idealistic and those who are realistic as to what can be accomplished. The idealistic are acting as though there are no sinners and everyone can do precisely what God expects of them. In other words, everyone can and should obey all the Ten Commandants all the time. The realistic, on the other hand, may well know what the ideal is, but know that we are incapable of living up to this. A realistic position accepts that we are broken, including all people of faith. Hence, in some instances, abortion may be a last resort, albeit a very reluctant last resort. This is the problem Paul had, as expressed in Romans 7:18–19, when he wrote: "I can will what is right, but I cannot do it. For I do not do the good I want, but the evil I do not want is what I do." Paul knew he was broken even as his ultimate hope was in Christ.

Conflict arises when the same people/groups are idealistic in some areas but realistic in others. They are inconsistent, as are all of us from time to time. Many Christians are resolutely anti-abortion (idealistic) but accept divorce (and remarriage) on pastoral grounds (realistic). No matter what justification may be provided for the latter under some circumstances, there is an inconsistency if no grounds are ever allowed for abortion—regardless of precipitating factors. A similar inconsistency is demonstrated when no sympathy is ever expressed for the actions of those with same-sex attraction, but there is far more acceptance for the divorce and remarriage of heterosexuals (see chapter 8). Once again, an uneasy mingling of idealism and realism comes to the surface. These examples are not intended to justify any of the positions referred to but to bring into the open the delicate balance needed when confronted with ethical (and sometimes scientific) dilemmas in very unsettling areas.

The question is how we live with each other in the face of such inconsistencies. For me, a fundamental postulate is the brokenness of the human condition. I always return to the question of what is the truest expression of biblical teaching, and especially the attitudes of Jesus and the fluidity of some of his actions, for example, in response to the woman taken in adultery (John 7:53—8:11) and the occasions when he healed on the Sabbath (John 5:1–18). This stands in contrast to the rigidity that the religious leaders of his day resorted to, a rigidity that some contemporary followers of Jesus are tempted to emulate.

What then of the science-faith debate, and research using those human embryos generally no longer required by couples in IVF programs? The idealist will undoubtedly contend that surplus embryos should never be produced in IVF programs, or that IVF should not be permitted. The reality within society is that IVF exists, and surplus embryos are produced and at some stage many will have to be discarded (see chapter 6 and 7). The decision-making then comes down to finding ways in which good can be elicited from evil (on the assumption that the destruction of embryos under these circumstances is deemed an evil). Strictly controlled research is being equated with destruction, in the same way as the benefits of IVF are equated with the negatives of producing an excess of embryos and as the life-saving goods of organ transplantation with the negatives of an untimely death. Arguments along these lines do not derive in any neat manner from Scripture. By the same token, there is no direct scriptural teaching to encourage or condemn research on surplus embryos. The one proviso is that the research is of high quality with a high probability of contributing to human well-being, and it will not demean human life, including prenatal human life.

Finding a Way Forward

I cannot pretend I have no biases. I am a scientist and a conservative Christian. Together these frame my hybrid culture, and it is within this culture that I function and from which I aim to speak to others in a host of different cultural and social contexts. Richard Mouw, professor of faith and public life at Fuller Theological Seminary in the United States and previously president of Fuller, writes: "There is nothing in this emphasis that undermines a commitment to biblical orthodoxy. But it does impress on us the need to be conscious of how all of our preaching and theologizing are inevitably contextualized. None of us escapes the formative influence of our cultural situation in our understanding of the biblical message."[8]

The temptation for theologically conservative Christians is to absolutize the cultural trappings surrounding their understanding of the faith on

8. Mouw, *Restless Faith*, 64–65.

the assumption that their understanding of it, even in contentious ethical areas, is the sole correct one. In contentious areas, Mouw uses the description of the "messiness of theology."[9] This is not an endorsement of fuzzy ideas but underlines the tentativeness of many applied positions that are in tension with one another. It demands a humility that recognizes that it is perfectly acceptable to be puzzled when engaging with ambiguities and conundrums, and learning how to disagree positively with brothers and sisters in Christ, and how to be perplexed together. When these are the terms of engagement, there is no room for caricatures, stereotypes, or derogatory labels.

I am at home in a form of Christianity that has well-defined borders and yet allows a large amount of freedom of thought and expression. This was well expressed by Vernon Grounds, onetime president of the Denver Seminary, when he wrote in 1965: "Here is no unanchored liberalism—freedom to think without commitment. Here is no encrusted dogmatism—commitment without the freedom to think. Here is vibrant Evangelicalism—freedom to think within the bounds laid down in Scripture."[10] I am keen to learn from a range of theologians even when some of their theological horizons are different from mine, and I have been able to benefit from some of their insights. These include the importance of valuing other humans on the ground that they are neighbors to be loved and Bonhoeffer's notion of the "penultimate" in addressing ethical imperatives.[11] For him, the penultimate looks at what is actually possible in a world that is not yet the perfect world of the future—the world of the ultimate. It is what I have been referring to as "realism."

Scientists writing in theological territory are always at something of a disadvantage. Of course, their grasp of the scientific evidence is far superior to that of the majority of theologians, but what is the driving force? Is it the theology or the science? In my view, the two should work hand-in-hand, but this is not always the case. If the duality is that of science and Scripture, it is clear that in many instances the biblical writers had little, if anything, to say about many of the contemporary complexities that deeply trouble us. This gap has to be filled in, and inevitably there will be a speculative tinge to it. This is where biblical scholars, theologians, and scientists have their respective roles to play. None of these will have all the answers, and none

---

9. Mouw, *Restless Faith*, 99, 123.

10. Quoted in Young, "Recapturing Evangelical Identity and Mission," 46–65, 58.

11. See Olson's summary of the significance of this distinction in "The 'Ultimate' and the 'Penultimate.'"

should give the impression that that is the case. Unfortunately, on occasion biblical scholars and theologians suggest otherwise, leaving no room for any significant input from scientists, even when the issues being debated have substantial scientific components. The opposite is also the case, when scientists make grandiose pronouncements allegedly based on solid science but lacking any nuanced ethical, let alone theological, input, and all-too-often subtly utilizing highly speculative notions.

My commitment to the scientific endeavor and my understanding that this endeavor is from God compel me to take serious note of the relevant science as I set about melding this with the theological directives at my disposal. To ignore scientific input is to intimate that, at best, scientific insights are superfluous and, at worst, unwanted. For a Christian like me, and for a scientist like me, this is unacceptable and does the Christian cause a grave disservice.

2

An Anatomist Confronts Ethics

Entering an Ethics-Free Zone as a Christian

ON MY ARRIVAL IN the University of Otago in Dunedin, New Zealand, in the early 1980s as a professor of anatomy, I had no inkling that this would cast me into an ethical quagmire. The general assumption was that anatomy was an ethics-free zone. It was sufficiently far removed from the daily ethical quandaries that faced clinicians as to be untouched by the messy realities of daily ethical decision-making. Its "quasi-patients" were dead, unable to complain or raise difficult objections to whatever anatomists and their students may do to them. No Christians that I knew raised objections to what went on in anatomy dissecting rooms, and as far as I could tell there was no theological literature on the subject. Silence surrounded anatomists and anatomists on the whole were happy to keep it that way.

There appeared to be no reason why I, as a Christian, should think any differently. For once, I was not entering contentious territory; this was quite different from abortion. I was not about to be vilified for my stance on anything because it seemed there was nothing to get me or anyone else into trouble. Everyone seemed to know what had gone on in anatomy schools in past centuries, such as their close association with the bodies of condemned criminals, their even more dubious involvement in digging up the graves of the recently deceased, and on a small number of occasions commissioning murders when the supply of bodies by these other means proved insufficient. In the 1980s little was known of the activities of anatomists in Germany and other Nazi territories in the 1930s and 1940s; light had not yet been cast upon the highly questionable liaisons between anatomists and the Nazi authorities. On the whole, the dubious record of anatomy and anatomists seemed to be confined to history and to be of little, if any, relevance to contemporary anatomists, let alone to Christians. There was little chance of Christians getting upset at my being an anatomist, even if some muttered under their breath that if I had become a medical practitioner, I could actually have helped living people.

And yet, I was far from satisfied. As I looked around me, I was beginning to see ethical issues everywhere. The bodies in the department had been donated, and yet this was far from typical practice in many anatomy departments across the world, where anatomists were dependent upon the availability of "unclaimed" bodies, generally those of murder victims or of those who had been abandoned and no longer had any family members. From my angle as a Christian this was totally unacceptable, since it pointed to deeply ingrained inequality within so many societies. The poor and unwanted, who had not consented to their bodies being used in this manner, ended up being used to educate students. This seemed to me to be unjust, even though at that stage I had given it little considered thought. On top of this, the department housed large collections of the skeletal remains of indigenous populations, both Māori and Pacific Islander. No one outside the department was aware of the extent of these collections; once again this struck me as demeaning to the living descendants of these people. I knew I had to do something to rectify what I was coming to recognize was an unjust state of affairs.

It would probably have remained that way for a few more years, except that my increasing awareness of ethical imperatives in responding to indigenous skeletal remains[1] led me to open discussions in 1993 with local Māori, informing them of the existence of this collection, inviting them to inspect it, and together aiming to seek a way forward. This happened over the next few years, and past wrongs were to a degree rectified; subsequent developments have led to a very positive relationship between biological anthropologists in the department and Māori throughout New Zealand.

The department also had, in its long-established museum, a collection of preserved dissected material and organs, plus fetuses and embryos from

---

1. My first paper on ways of approaching indigenous skeletal remains appeared in 1998: Jones and Harris, "Archeological Human Remains: Scientific, Cultural and Ethical Considerations," 253–64.

the early part of the twentieth century. These were used to varying degrees in teaching, but by today's standards had not been obtained with appropriate consent. Decisions had to be taken on what was to be done with this material; to dispose of it, continue to use it, or leave it in storage. These were typical museum archives of anonymous archival material, and I had to determine what was an ethical means of dealing with this material.[2]

And then I was confronted with the manner in which the department obtained brains for neuroanatomy classes, a transaction in which I had a personal and professional interest. The brains were obtained at postmortem and came directly to the anatomy department from the pathology department. I gave no thought to the ethical niceties of this informal trade and whether the family of the deceased had given their permission for the removal of the brain. For me the transfer of brains from one department to another was innocuous, and the notion of informed consent had not at that time entered my lexicon. Human brains had been obtained in this way for many years, and no one had raised any concerns: it was not a contentious matter, and the brains were being used for good purposes. Neither had I, at that stage, been introduced to the concept of moral complicity. All this was to change a few years later in the light of the 1988 Cartwright Inquiry in New Zealand, stemming as it did from research carried out on human patients without their knowledge, let alone consent.[3] The emerging debate on the role of informed consent in clinical medicine had profound ramifications both at the clinical and preclinical levels. From my vantage point as a Christian, the social and ethical concerns raised by these developments stimulated me to engage theologically with the issues they were raising as I came to recognize that they would benefit from Christian reflection.

A Discipline with Unethical Foundations

It gradually dawned on me that I was a Christian practicing a profession based on highly suspect ethical foundations. Many of my predecessors in anatomy acted in appallingly unethical fashion, sometimes by the standards of their day but in other cases by any standards. As an anatomist I had the dubious distinction of having to reflect on ethical developments against the background of a discipline with an unsavory past. This was no ivory tower exercise, since I was a representative of a somewhat questionable discipline.

2. See Jones, Gear, and Galvin, "Stored Human Tissue," 343–47.
3. Cartwright Inquiry, *The Report of the Committee of Inquiry*.

No longer was I able to escape from ethical debate and even conflict. Moreover, it was my Christian convictions that forced me to confront unjust and inequitable practices, and that led to the conviction that I should aim to rectify these as much as I could in the present.

This realization first came into prominence in the late 1980s and early 1990s when I began advocating for the primacy of the bequest of bodies to anatomy departments for dissection rather than regarding the use of unclaimed bodies as the norm. This trajectory had begun to change in the 1960s. Unfortunately, welcome as this change was from my angle, it took place largely for pragmatic reasons and with little ethical deliberation. As social circumstances had gradually changed, with a decrease in vagrants (including those housed long-term in mental institutions) whose bodies had provided rich pickings for anatomists, the supply had to be augmented, and this is where bequests came to the fore. Sadly, anatomists' attitudes had not changed, and they were not acting out of high-minded ethical concern for the downtrodden. They were ensuring they had a reliable supply of bodies for dissection classes.[4]

This debate between the use of unclaimed bodies versus the use of bequests is not an arbitrary one; it goes to the heart of the tensions that arise between science and ethics. There will inevitably be tensions at this interface as scientists strive to push back the frontiers of knowledge with as few impediments as possible. In this case, anatomists would like to have at their disposal human bodies of "high quality," that is, in as fresh a state as possible, and the younger the better. It takes little imagination to realize that this is rarely going to be achievable with routine bequests, where the majority of bodies are those of the elderly. Anatomists have usually had to live with this limitation and have accepted it. But in the 1930s and 1940s a cataclysmic series of events took place, namely, when the Third Reich reigned supreme in Germany and neighboring countries such as Austria. Senior anatomists were sympathetic to the regime and worked closely with Nazi officials to obtain numerous high-quality bodies sourced from the gas chambers. On some occasions death was timed to suit the requirements of the anatomists, with the victims being chosen to match the requests of the

---

4. My mature reflection on this matter led to what I regard as my definitive publication advocating for the use of bequests alone. See Jones and Whitaker. "Anatomy's Use of Unclaimed Bodies: Reasons Against Continued Dependence on an Ethically Dubious Practice," 246–54. A broader overview of these developments can be found in chapter 1 of my book with Maja Whitaker, *Speaking for the Dead: The Human Body in Biology and Medicine*.

anatomists. This was the ghastly nadir of the use of unclaimed bodies, but its horror demonstrated that anatomists were capable of unremitting evil even in the mid-twentieth century. The title of Sabine Hildebrandt's book, *The Anatomy of Murder*, encapsulates the depths to which the anatomical profession sank in those years and in that regime.[5] For me the realization that these events took place a mere twenty to thirty years before I embarked on anatomy as a career was sobering. Unfortunately, the same comment would have applied if I had been a medical practitioner, another profession that sank to unimaginable depths during the Nazi regime.

True, this is an extreme example, but it provides a salutary reminder of what can happen when unclaimed bodies are available for use by anatomists; from a Christian angle this is the apotheosis of evil. It is also a reminder that new challenges are emerging repeatedly for anatomists. There are many such challenges, including the sale of bodies and body parts as commercially valuable goods, the display of dissected bodies in large public exhibitions, and the ready availability of digitized images of human tissue on YouTube and social media (see below).

When I started to show an interest in the ethical issues in anatomy, I was looked upon with benign amusement. More sinisterly, a few concluded that this emanated from my Christian worldview, and that I was intent on infiltrating the science of anatomy with Christian propaganda. Phrased differently, the purity of science was being contaminated by the prejudice of religion. The longing on the part of some was to view anatomy as an ethically neutral, rigidly scientific discipline. Its goal was to impart to students the well-worn facts of human anatomy, unencumbered by any hint of humanity or any suggestion that the means of obtaining dead human bodies may not always have been ethical. There was no acknowledgement that anatomy needs direction, a direction that was going to come from bioethics, with its input from secular sources as well as a host of religious ones. I was beginning to challenge this notion of neutrality and in time this led to what I regard as a new subdiscipline, the ethics of anatomy. As in so many cases, developments like this are not ostensibly Christian, and yet the thrust behind them may have a strong Christian element; that was certainly the case here.

As I have indicated, those in the discipline of anatomy would, until recently, not have troubled themselves with ethical debate. What they did with, and to, dead human bodies was legal, and hence there appeared to be no need for ethical input. They did not have to bother themselves with the

---

5. Hildebrandt, *The Anatomy of Murder*.

uncertain values and value systems of those in the humanities, nor even of those working in clinical medicine. The apparent assurance of these attitudes, prevalent in Western anatomy departments up to the 1980s and beyond, was bought at a price, that of ignoring the history of the discipline and the numerous vicissitudes through which it had come, many of which were deeply unethical with ongoing repercussions for the health of anatomy.

Emergence of Anatomy as a Science

These comments have begun to unravel a few features of the background to modern anatomy and to my growing interest in its ethical foundations. It has also started to demonstrate why I have seen this as a Christian venture, and why there is a close relationship between how my Christian faith has driven my interests as a scientist.

The move into modern science carried with it the demand that ideas are based on hard evidence, what can be seen with the eyes and touched with the hands, that is, on observation and experimentation. Data have to be obtained from real life and not simply from reading books that, in turn, are based on ideas that have been promulgated for years if not centuries. And this was just as important in human anatomy as anywhere else. However, even minimal reflection shows that when the human body is the object of interest, the actual human body itself has to be examined, pulled apart, and analyzed. Before this could be accepted as a legitimate (and ethical) practice, a transformation in cultural and religious attitudes had to occur, struggles that were seen most clearly in Western societies. After all, dissecting the human body is akin to dissecting *my* body; it could be *me*. The personal element in this is stark; it is of a completely different magnitude from dissecting an animal, let alone investigating anything in geology, astronomy, or laser physics.

Imagine the extent of the change in attitudes demanded of societies in the past when faced with a proposal of dissecting an actual dead human being. Instead of burying the dead body of your loved one in a grave in consecrated ground, to rest "peacefully" and in a dignified manner, it went to strangers in a medical school to be "cut up" ("anatomized" was the phrase used) and deconstructed. There is little wonder that people were horrified, horror made all the worse by the lengths to which the anatomists of the time went in order to obtain this precious material. As so often happens in science, the scientists were attempting to move into territory that was uncharted and generally unwelcome. By the standards of their day, they were acting suspiciously and unethically. This is seen clearly in the activities of "the father of modern anatomy," Andreas Vesalius (1514-64).

His insistence in the sixteenth century on studying and dissecting the human body was a move into dubious territory, and a move away from studying animals and relying upon the pivotal and ultimately moribund writings of his Greek forebear, Galen (130-200 CE). Unfortunately for Galen, he did not have access to human bodies (denied to him in the Roman Empire) and hence relied upon dissecting animals, and on a number of occasions, this led to misleading data and concepts. In spite of these errors, he was responsible for restructuring the body of medical knowledge, a staggering achievement that was, unfortunately, accompanied by a tragedy: his concepts remained unchallenged for 1,300 years. During this long period, human dissection disappeared from view, because Galen's observations and interpretations were accepted as correct. They had taken on the mantle of "holy writ"; they could not be challenged. As they had acquired the status of holy writ, there was no need to challenge them; what Galen had written was accurate and consequently had to be accepted. He had dissected the "body," and so any further experimentation was redundant. Since no one else had done this, the stagnation continued until the fourteenth century.

The environment within which these early dissections were carried out was hostile and tended to be carried out in secret and spasmodically. Few advances in anatomical understanding were being made, but gradually permission was given by a number of European universities for dissection to be undertaken. This new atmosphere owed a great deal to a range of people with their scientific and artistic abilities, including Leonardo da Vinci (1452-1519), and served as a prelude to the majestic work of Andreas Vesalius in the sixteenth century. It was Vesalius who cast off all vestiges of the Galenic tradition, and set modern anatomy on a firm footing, but only by dissecting actual human bodies. But where did the bodies come from? Being novel, there had to be a novel supply chain, and this was from graveyards. This meant challenging conventions and religious strictures. There was no other way in which the burgeoning discipline of anatomy could acquire a scientific footing. But was this ethical? By contemporary standards the answer is no, but that would have been a non-question in the sixteenth century. He probably had no choice.

What is a Christian to make of this? In one regard it is impossible for me to comment, since I live in a completely different social, cultural, and religious space. The biblical injunction against stealing provides no place for stealing bodies, and yet you could argue that this was done in the hope of ultimately benefiting others through anatomical research. In practice little of this justification would have been appreciated or understood by anyone at the time. I have to accept that it was done with good intentions within a context totally foreign to us today. However, the contrast between Vesalius and the anatomists of the Nazi era is helpful. Vesalius was moving in uncharted territory, whereas these latter-day anatomists were indulging in grossly unethical practices for their own benefit. I have sympathy with Vesalius, but find the Nazi anatomists reprehensible.

The reality is that knowledge of the human body cannot be acquired from reflection alone. Science is analysis and experimentation, and while ethical analysis is crucial, it cannot be undertaken in isolation of the science that gives rise to the need for this analysis in the first place. Investigations, such as those of Vesalius, have to start somewhere, and the starting point will invariably be tentative, probing where no one has previously probed and frequently using material that no one had access to before or had not thought of accessing. The justification for Vesalius was revolutionary research, and while this is not justification in itself, it sets it apart from the grave robbers of the eighteenth and early nineteenth centuries who were obtaining bodies for teaching and for enriching their own (private) medical schools.

This is a world removed from how bodies are obtained in most places today, but it is surprisingly relevant for Christians. While no Christians today will be faced with precisely these challenges, this move into unrecognizable territory occurs repeatedly in science. As with the emergence of modern anatomy, it breaks barriers and raises uncomfortable questions. From today's perspective, it broke all the ethical rules—no informed consent, indeed no consent of any description. And yet Vesalius was in unknown territory, as is so often the case with ground-breaking science. Some of today's Christians are frequently critical of new developments in science, and this incident serves as a reminder that negativity may not always be the appropriate initial response.

Just as Vesalius was a man of his time and cultural climate, Henry Gray of *Gray's Anatomy* fame was much the same in the 1850s. The pictures that dominated the first edition of what became known as *Gray's Anatomy* were based on bodies dissected at St. George's Hospital in London, bodies that would have come from the poor, dying alone in workhouses, prisons, and hospitals. All these would have been unclaimed, and some may have arrived in the anatomy department as a result of deception. In no way does this denigrate Gray's contribution to anatomy, but it places it in its historic context.[6] He could not have acted differently as long as he wanted to dissect bodies and produce a text based on actual dissections. It is helpful to reiterate this point by referring to a contrast, once again that of Nazi anatomists, in this instance Eduard Pernkopf (1888–1955). With his collaborators Pernkopf produced a superb anatomical atlas, in which the majestic diagrams are based on dissections carried out on political prisoners put to death in the gas chambers. As an ardent Nazi, he was fully aware of the origin of the bodies, and he and his artists showed this by using Nazi symbols in some of the atlas' plates. This detestable behavior is in sharp contrast to that of the ground-breaking work of Henry Gray. While there was a clear demarcation between the ethical expectations of the 1850s and the 1930s–1940s, the most fundamental ethical norms were unchanged—murder was murder in both periods. Henry Gray was not implicated in murder; Eduard Pernkof was.

An unwritten assumption in this discussion is that, from a Christian perspective, the body is worth taking seriously. There are examples in Scripture of the dead body and bones of the dead being treated with respect; they were not to be desecrated (Amos 2:1–3). Joseph requested that his bones were to be taken to Canaan at this death (Gen 50:22–26; Exod 13:19), while Jesus's followers tended his body after his death, and ensured that his body was laid in a tomb (Matt 27:57–61; Mark 15:42—16:2). For Paul, the resurrection body was viewed as a physical one (1 Cor 15:42–52; 1 Thess 4:13–18). While not identical to the mortal body, this will have sufficient similarities to warrant the term "body."

This points to a fundamental difference in a Christian response, namely, that it contains within it a future orientation not found in general ethical stances. The body is a reminder of the ongoing dimensions of human existence as well as of our mortality. And so, to value the dead body is to value the person and to see that person as one who mirrors God. Hence, to devalue the dead body is to devalue those still alive and also to question the purposes and intentions of God in creating people in his image.

The Trajectory from Use of Unclaimed Bodies to Bequests

I started thinking seriously about where the department's bodies came from in the very early 1990s, with studies examining the source of bodies from

6. Richardson, *The Making of Mr Gray's Anatomy*.

the late nineteenth century to the present time. This revealed that they had been unclaimed all the way through to the late 1950s, initially the bodies of those with no relatives or friends and latterly those of long-term patients in mental hospitals. That provided the data, but what was I to make of it? And what was I to make of it as a Christian?

Bodies such as these, the so-called "unclaimed bodies," provided the majority of bodies for anatomical departments throughout the world. There was no one to care for these people following their death, and of course there was no informed consent. The use of bodies such as these can be traced back to the early nineteenth century in the United Kingdom, when pivotal legislation legitimizing this practice was passed as the 1832 Anatomy Act. In all probability this reflected negative social attitudes towards the poor and disadvantaged. The medical profession was firmly of the opinion that the preferable source of bodies for dissection was to be found in hospitals: the bodies of those dying alone or whose families were too poor to provide for them at death. The inevitable result was that poverty became the sole criterion for dissection. It is unfortunate that under the aegis of the unclaimed bodies mantra, deception and a cruel disregard for the feelings and concerns of families grieving the loss of a loved one have appeared repeatedly. Time and again, the drive for an adequate supply of bodies tended to override all other considerations.

There was no ill intent in moving in this direction, but it was deficient ethically and, I would claim, deficient from a Christian angle. It also opened up the possibility of being used in evil ways never contemplated by those anatomists and legislators of the early nineteenth century. As already indicated, the evil came to light in the 1930s and 1940s during the Nazi regime. At that time members of the medical profession, including anatomists, were intimately involved in experimentation on human subjects. The crux of the tragedy was that bodies, especially high-quality bodies, that is, bodies of the young, including some with congenital abnormalities, became readily available from concentration camps. To make them even more attractive, the bodies could be made available shortly after death. These bodies were unclaimed, although that is to use the term in a very questionable sense.

Once again, what comes to the fore is the conflict between that which is scientifically ideal (high-quality bodies) and that which respects human considerations. The anatomists involved in this enterprise made the deaths of concentration camp inmates part of their research design. They became agents of evil as their reductionist and materialist view of the meaning of human life came to control their actions. These extremes are not the inevitable end result of the ability to use unclaimed bodies; but they do provide a sobering lesson in that it is a model of body acquisition that lacks ethical safeguards.

Legitimizing unclaimed bodies as a source of bodies for dissection, and viewing it as the routine source of bodies, has exposed the anatomy profession to moral turpitude. It has allowed anatomists to ignore the cultural inequities within societies and has provided them with *carte blanche* to exploit those occupying less privileged strata than the ones they themselves occupied. Attitudes of this nature would have been avoided had anatomists lived by a value system based on the equality of all peoples regardless of their status within society. My Christian faith has compelled me to advocate for equality, and therefore protection of the poor, the long-term mentally ill, many indigenous groups, and in general the downtrodden and disadvantaged in society. At one time or another, the bodies of all these groups have been utilized by anatomists for purely pragmatic reasons. It is only bequest programs with inbuilt rigorous standards of informed consent that have protected the vulnerable and have opened the way to what I would describe as practices that align with Christian aspirations.

It is because of this that I have been in the forefront of moves to replace all remaining systems based on the use of unclaimed bodies with bequests. My first efforts in this direction in the mid-1990s at an anatomical conference were met with strong disagreement by one anatomist from an Asian country. Her reasoning was that these derelicts had served no useful purpose during life, but that had changed at death, with the availability of their bodies for dissection and medical education. Their dead bodies were worth far more than their lives had been. I could follow her reasoning, but was appalled by the notion that an individual had contributed nothing at all during life, no matter how lowly their place in society. For me that said a great deal about the nature of that society and its acceptance of the meaninglessness of some people's lives.

The basis to the argument that the dead body has an intrinsic value that cannot be totally separated from the value ascribed to the person when alive has Christian roots. We disrespect a recently deceased person when we dissect that person's body without their consent either prior to death or without the approval of close family and friends to represent their interests after death. In the absence of such consent, we are free to exploit them and use them for our own purposes. This is the antithesis of the teachings of Jesus and of the ways in which he dealt with the people he encountered, especially those considered of little value within his own society, and even those of another culture such as the Samaritans (Luke 10:25–37; John 4:1–26).

Unfortunately, it would be misleading to give the impression that all is straightforward, since there remain many societies where cultural considerations militate against moving in the bequest direction. The acceptance of body donation and dissection in Western countries has been hard won and a long, drawn-out process. It has also been made easier by the secularization of these societies. While Christian thinkers have not been implacably opposed to dissection, acceptance of it has been largely muted. The days of burying the bodies of the dead in consecrated ground have largely disappeared, and cremation has been generally accepted. However, these trends have drifted in rather than been actively debated and approved. The result is that body donation and subsequent dissection are approved within Christian circles almost as much as within other sections of the community. It has become a non-issue, but like a number of other ethical questions its acceptance has largely been by default.

The same cannot be said of other cultures within the West and even more so in non-Western parts of the world. This comes in the form of a desire to ensure that the dead body is buried intact, with no organs removed. While the reasoning behind this stance varies between cultures, the implications for body dissection (and in some situations organ donation) are the same. No dissection is acceptable. The dead body represents an important link in the family's history and ongoing trajectory or has a vital role to play in retaining connections with one's ancestors. Either way, body donation is frowned upon.

These responses raise a number of challenges for Christian anatomists. Assuming they themselves have no problem with body donation and subsequent dissection, they are called to respect and value the views of those groups with different perspectives, no matter how much they may disagree with the rationale or religious worldview underlying these perspectives. Respect demands treating others as deserving the same sensitivities as we ourselves expect to be shown. This is implicit within a Christian response and is to be grounded in the response of Christian anatomists.

Until recent times anatomists tended to act in a superior fashion, expecting others to channel "unwanted" bodies to anatomy departments. This came through to me in a stark manner when visiting a city in another country where there were large numbers of murders over most weekends. These bodies fell under the aegis of the city pathologist, who was given a torrid time by some of the local anatomists for not passing these on directly to the local anatomy department. They appeared to pay little attention to the fact that this was outside his control, let alone that it lacked informed consent and paid no attention to the feelings of the grieving families. To make matters worse many of these victims would have been black, in contrast to the anatomists, who were white. As a Christian I am constantly reminded of the teaching and example of Jesus for whom any indication of superiority, whether cultural, racial, professional, religious, or personal, was anathema and totally alien to the kingdom of God. Anatomists are to serve others, their students, researchers, and the public and are never to act as though they have a right to dissect the bodies of others. They function on the basis of mutual agreement and respect.

The differences between, for instance, Muslim and Buddhist cultures regarding body donation should impress upon anatomists the centrality of gaining insight into the religious and cultural settings within which they are functioning and the importance of understanding the culture and its relevance for their interests in the science of the dead human body. There may be no simple resolution to what at first sight is an impasse for them in their search for bequests, and the challenge is to find ethically and religiously acceptable alternatives. This entails serious engagement with ethical and religious reasoning, leading to dialogue with those holding different religious and cultural perspectives from their own scientific/materialist ones. There is no room for any form of superiority, a position eminently at one with Christian attitudes.

Displaying Dead Bodies in Public

Up to this juncture, I have confined my attention to what is considered to be traditional anatomy: wet tissue fixed in formalin or some variant of this. This is the usual picture one has of anatomy in a teaching environment. But what if bodies were to be prepared in quite a different way, and the dead bodies were to be displayed in revolutionary new ways? And what if the bodies were to be used for a purpose other than educating health science students? What if they were to be prepared in such a manner that they could be displayed in life-like form to the general public?[7] Would this intro-

---

7. See a 2016 assessment of mine: "The Public Display of Plastinates as a Challenge to the Integrity of Anatomy," 46–54.

duce additional ethical queries, and would it directly challenge Christian beliefs and assumptions?

These questions have been asked repeatedly over the past thirty years, ever since public exhibitions of plastinated and dissected bodies appeared on the scene in the late 1980s. During the process of plastination water is removed from the tissue and is replaced by epoxy resins. This converts wet, smelly tissue into odorless, dry material that can be handled with ease. The tissue can also be molded into various configurations, meaning that the dissected body can be displayed in upright poses to resemble someone running, playing football, performing as a ballerina, or sitting down and playing chess. The results are dramatic and are massively different from the picture we normally have of a dead corpse lying horizontal on a slab in a cold dissecting room or pathologist's laboratory. These plastinated bodies do not look dead, even though they have been dissected; they are presented so that they look alive and are actually participating in activities we generally associate with the living and the healthy. There may be a decided element of deception here, but should this worry us?

Does this process and this way of displaying dead bodies have any relevance for Christians? When a number of church leaders have heard about these exhibitions (*BodyWorlds* is the best known) they have reacted negatively. The reason given is that the body is sacred, and that these shows dishonor the body and threaten the dignity of human beings. It is claimed that they stem from a materialist worldview. Comments along these lines tend to come from those with a more fundamentalist mind set; other religious voices are more open to acknowledging that increased understanding and knowledge of the human body can have benefits leading to a greater appreciation of our dignity as human beings.[8]

As an anatomist I find myself struggling to understand the basis of the negative comments, unless all dissection and all study of the dead human body is opposed. Are the objections based on our sensibilities being offended, and if so, do these have a reliable religious base? When these bodies have been donated to the organizations mounting the exhibitions, what theological reasons are there to object to public displays of dissected and plastinated bodies? Is it the process of plastination that is objectionable, or is it the display of the bodies and body parts? I am aware that I may be biased since, I have been thoroughly inculcated into the world of dead bodies

---

8. This section is based on my 2016 article: "The Artificial World of Plastination: A Challenge to Religious Perspectives on the Dead Human Body."

and their dissection for teaching and research purposes. But I have also lived with the science and theology around these practices for many years.

We still need to come back to the question posed by plastination and the public display of plastinated bodies. A starting point is provided by comparing this process to other ways in which we routinely treat dead bodies—bury them or cremate them. There is relatively little discussion of the merits of the two in Western Christian circles. However, this has not always been the case. The church fathers held an unfavorable view of cremation, a view that was to continue for many years into the future. For them, it was a pagan act, a view of cremation that became the default position of later theologians, including the Protestant Reformers. It was not until the twentieth century that opposition began to relax, although it remains a disputed position in some quarters.

From Cremation to Plastination

For some, cremation is what is described as a disputable issue.[9] Scripture is silent on the specifics of how to treat the deceased, although the body is theologically significant. The overall trajectory of biblical examples is in a pro-burial direction. This is because the biblical characters showed great care and respect for the bodies of their loved ones. Examples from the Old Testament include Abraham and the burial of Sarah (Gen 23:3–18), with Abraham himself being buried (Gen 25:9), as well as Isaac and Rebekah (Gen 35:29; 49:31) and Jacob and Leah (Gen 50:13). Additionally, there are many other examples of burial, including Rachel (Gen 35:19–20), Joseph (Gen 50:25; Exod 13:19; Josh 24:32), Aaron (Deut 10:6), Moses (Deut 34:5–8), Joshua (Josh 24:30), Samuel (1 Sam 25:1), and David (1 Kgs 2:10). Moving into the New Testament one encounters the burials of John the Baptist (Matt 14:12), Lazarus (John 11:17–18), and Stephen (Acts 8:2). Preeminently, Jesus's body was placed in a tomb (John 19:38–42). Over against these burial illustrations, a possible counter-illustration of cremation is found in the book of Amos. In this case, Amos condemned those who had unleashed their venom on the body of one of their enemies by burning to ashes the bones of Edom's king (Amos 2:1–3). This, however, was desecration of his dead body, and so the condemnation was of abuse of the body and not cremation.

---

9. Jones, "To Bury or Burn? Toward an Ethic of Cremation," 335–47.

There seems little doubt that these examples in Scripture suggest that the dead body was respected. For instance, Joseph did not want his mortal remains left in Egypt, the land of captivity, following his death (Gen 50:22–26; Exod 13:19). Even if this was symbolic, it points towards the idea that the dead body is sufficiently important to be treated respectfully by others. Following the death of Jesus, his followers tended his body (Matt 27:57–61; Mark 15:42—16:2; Luke 23:50—24:1; John 19:38–42) and considered it inappropriate to leave his body on the cross, especially over the Sabbath day. Joseph of Arimathea ensured that Jesus's body was laid in his own new tomb, following which a group of his followers ensured that it was anointed with spices and then bound in accordance with Jewish custom.

These illustrations take us a little way, but admittedly it is only a little way. The theological considerations raised in the burial-cremation conversation center on the dignity of the human body and the future bodily resurrection. Of even greater importance, both focus on the central significance of the human body for our lives as creatures created in God's image. Human beings are embodied creatures who experience nothing and relate to no one apart from our bodily senses. It is far from misleading to say that we are our bodies since we cease to exist as mortal beings when our bodies cease to function. In his incarnation, Jesus experienced what it was like to be human, with the limitations and fragility of a human body. In doing this, he imbued the body with dignity and elevated it to a position of respect and worth. But what about after death; does the significance of the body diminish along with decay of the body?

The future bodily resurrection builds on the biblical teaching that human beings cannot exist apart from the body, even in the future life after death. Paul was clear: the resurrection is a physical one (1 Cor 15:42–52; 1 Thess 4:13–18). Our present mortal bodies will be transformed into resurrection bodies, one form will be transformed into another form; the picture of the transformation of acorns into oak trees encapsulates this thought nicely. The term "resurrected bodies" suggests they will be far more like our present bodies than ethereal spirits. After his resurrection, Jesus had a body that was recognizable to those who knew him.

Respecting the Body

All this suggests that our present bodies should be respected. This future dimension imbues a Christian perspective with a dimension missing from secular ones; one that sets it apart from all secular ones, with its recognition that what we do to bodies now has ongoing repercussions. Not only this, if our bodies constitute the one common strand between what we are now and what we will become in the future, the prior wishes of the deceased should be respected and taken very seriously.

What, then, about the process of plastination? Central to the Christian gospel is the belief that believers will one day be resurrected in a glorified, physical body (1 Cor 15:20). In light of this, does it matter whether the "body" to be transformed at the resurrection is recently deceased and decaying, has been dead for many years and has decayed, or has been preserved and continues to exist in a plastinated state? Inevitably, these questions take us into highly speculative territory, far removed from any direct biblical input. No matter what one makes of this process and of the ongoing identification of the preserved individual, two points stand out. The first is that deceased, preserved individuals are no longer able to contribute to the community of which they were previously an integral part, including the Christian community. No matter what form their body now takes, they are dead. The second is that when it comes to the transformation of the dead body into the resurrection body, the form of the dead body is irrelevant in theological terms. What is significant is the quality and character of the life lived by the person now deceased.

But are dead bodies automatically devalued by being placed on display in public exhibitions when they have consented to being displayed in this way? What is it about these displays that lead to these conclusions?

Plastination is a relatively modern phenomenon, emanating from the late 1980s, even though there are historical precedents. Assuming that the individuals whose bodies have been plastinated after their death gave their permission for this to happen prior to their death, there do not appear to be any major theological reasons for objecting to the process of plastination. Similarly for those whose bodies have been used in anatomy classes. This is where informed consent comes into its own. On the other hand, if the bodies are unclaimed, and, even worse, if the bodies are those condemned to death for political or religious reasons, the individuals' interests have been severely flouted.

When those whose bodies appear in public plastination exhibitions have consented to this specific use of their body following death, the display is not being disrespectful to those individuals. But what about those viewing the bodies? If it is an educational experience in which they, as members of the general public, learn about the organization of the human body, that may be a commendable action on their part. It may also lead them to dwell on the wonder of the body as God's creation. On the other hand, if their aim is to seek some voyeuristic experience, that may amount to an exploitation of those on display. Overall, therefore, any exhibition will have different impacts on different people, leading to approval in some cases and disapproval in others.

The emphases and marketing of the organizers may well prove decisive in this regard, and this may be the crux of the debate from a Christian angle. The extent to which the bodies of the deceased are employed to entertain others, possibly in exhibitionist ways, comes close to demeaning those whose bodies are on display. It gives the distinct impression of utilizing bodies for gain, even if there is an educational component. Consequently, a Christian approach will seek to affirm the dignity and ongoing value of the bodies and will look guardedly at the manner in which they are displayed and the messages and images accompanying the marketing of the exhibitions. There is little doubt that from time to time there have been excesses, and some exhibits have had no educational merit. Such instances are highly problematic, even if there has been prior consent.

Public exhibitions of human bodies and human material are, by their very nature, commercial enterprises. This does not constitute grounds for condemning them, since substantial costs have been incurred in undertaking the dissections and the plastination. However, this increases the potential for turning the human exhibits into a means of financial gain. This may not be inevitable, but greed becomes a temptation. Enormous care is required to retain a healthy balance between educational and entertainment rationales and between respect and disrespect.

Christians in Anatomy

The illustrations I have touched on in this chapter have provided a glimpse into the multifaceted world of human anatomy and the many avenues calling out for Christian involvement. The wonder of God's creation revealed in the organization and functioning of the human body is readily taken for granted by all of us, including human anatomists. It works amazingly well most of the time in most people, and it is only when something is amiss that we are brought face-to-face with its intricacies and delicate operations. Our gratitude then turns to the health professionals who seek to rectify what has gone wrong.

All too often, though, we overlook the providence of God, his goodness in overseeing its remarkable efficiency, and the human creativity and ingenuity that have led to means of combatting illness and disease (chapters 3–5). God cooperates with human beings, from anatomists to pathologists, from epidemiologists to surgeons, from nurses to carers. None of this ignores the scientific mechanisms postulated to act in the body's functioning, nor in ways in which humans in their present form came into being. What it does is place these investigations into the wider context of his oversight and care for humankind.

As anatomists dissect the body in order to understand its intimate relationships and structure, they should never forget the body in its wholeness and completeness. As they peer into tissues and cells, they are never to lose sight of the organs and body systems of which these are a part and of the body in its completeness—the functioning human individual. Christians are to recognize God's goodness in the delicate balance within, and interrelationships of, the human body in all the dimensions they are privileged to investigate. Being an anatomist is a privilege, no matter how ethically contested the discipline may have been in its early stages, and the welter of ongoing questions that have to be addressed.

3

A Scientist's View of a Pandemic

Intersections of Science and Faith

MUCH OF THIS BOOK was written during the COVID-19 pandemic, leading to a major perturbation of many features of the world as we know it. This has raised a plethora of questions for Christians about how God works, how he protects his people, whether a cataclysmic event of this nature is God's judgment on rebellious mankind, and what (if any) role science has to play in combatting the worst aspects of the pandemic. As a Christian I have been forced to ask the degree to which science should be looked to as an instrument made available by God to heal the brokenness brought about by the virus responsible for the pandemic. The tragedy is that the religious and scientific perspectives can be viewed as diametric opposites, according to which only one is valid to the exclusion of the other. As I shall attempt to demonstrate, this is a distinctly unchristian approach as well as being counter-productive.

In the early stages of the pandemic in 2020, many Christians asked whether this was a manifestation of God's judgment on a sinful and recalcitrant people. Others wondered why a loving God, who has the whole world in his hands, had allowed this particular virus to mutate and become an unguided missile of biological warfare. In other words, there was the assumption that the origins of the coronavirus lay entirely within God's control, leading to the conclusion that the present scourge was a manifestation of God's displeasure with the pride and arrogance of the nations. The take-home message was that this was a warning to the church to change its ways and live in a manner far more pleasing to God. Some referred to the pandemic as a "bitter providence," that it was God shouting at us through physical misery, and that it was a call to realign our lives with the infinite worth of Christ.[1]

Some Christians put a different twist on the unfolding events, emphasizing that much of the mayhem was due to a lack of human wisdom, human self-centeredness, and human folly on the part of the leaders of societies. The trouble with this view was that every country had been caught up in the chaos and tragedy of decisions made far away from them and often none of their doing. Either way, the finger was pointed at those who were displeasing to God.

Interestingly, though, this was not a universal response among theologians. N. T. (Tom) Wright for one appeared to reject this thinking, which for him was nothing more than a knee-jerk and barely Christian response. In responding like this, he ruffled a few feathers, and yet it soon became apparent that his position, based on the biblical tradition of lament, was to prove far more practical and powerful. He pointed to the well-established tradition of lamentation found predominantly in the Psalms (Pss 6, 10, 13, 22).

The mystery of the biblical story is that God also laments. Some Christians like to think of God as above all the mess and chaos, knowing everything, in charge of everything, calm and unaffected by the troubles in his world. But that is not the picture provided in the Bible. Wright concluded that "it is no part of the Christian vocation to be able to explain what's happening and why. In fact, it *is* part of the Christian vocation *not to be able* to explain—and to lament instead."[2] His argument is that we are to become transformed into oases revealing the presence and healing love of God. As we lament, we are to demonstrate kindness and hope and utilize the fruits of emerging scientific understanding.

These thoughts provide an opening into seeing the pandemic in new light, through new eyes, in which scientific and religious inputs work in harmony, each contributing to the strengths of the other. For instance, the Psalms have played an enormous role in the church's response, especially during many months of lockdowns in one country after another. For instance, we learn from Psalm 91:1–2 that the shadow of the Almighty is a

---

1. Piper, *Coronavirus and Christ*.

2. Wright, "Christianity Offers No Answers about the Coronavirus. It's Not Supposed To."

place of refuge and safety, where we are to rest. But as we trust, we must also take our responsibilities seriously, for the benefit of our communities, our societies, and our world. The challenge is to bring the shadows of our anxieties and concerns into the shelter and shadow of the One who is in control and in whom we can trust.

For me, the pandemic immediately raised questions about the relationship between science and faith, a relationship brought to the fore in an unmistakable way. Any hint that this relationship may be of mere theoretical interest disappeared overnight. Nothing could be more practical and immediate; it is, quite literally, a life and death issue as well as of major theological significance. Questions raised about the relevance of God in a pandemic, or quite simply where is God in a pandemic, cannot be avoided. They are real heart-felt questions, easier to ask than to answer. And they are immensely practical questions.

For most people living in the West, the dimensions of a pandemic are novel, with their threat to destroy people and ravage communities, and in the first year (2020) the most we could do was employ what seem like primitive methods: keeping people apart, locking them down and caging them like unruly animals. Unsophisticated as these approaches may have appeared, what tools did we have to combat this novel threat to which there was initially no technological answer? The most that science could offer at that point were measures frequently downplayed even within the medical tool box, namely, public health measures and epidemiology. But even these measures, primitive as they may have seemed, suggested that the way to cope with the pandemic was by using scientifically-based weapons rather than what gave the appearance of spiritually-based approaches. Was this a way forward that Christians would accept, or would they object because science represented a secular (ungodly) response? These are fundamental science-faith duopolies which bring into the open the way in which Christians think about science and its place in God's world.

Medical Science as the Hand of God

My basic postulate is that medical science is the hand of God at work in a fallen world. God's purposes on the one hand and epidemiology and public health advice on the other complement each other; and in no sense are they mutually exclusive. These are all God-given directions, and we ignore them at our peril. Francis Collins, a committed Christian, discoverer of the genetic basis of cystic fibrosis (CF) and until the end of 2021 director of the National Institutes of Health (NIH) in the United States, is adamant that science is a gift from God, and the curiosity that we have to understand how the universe works can inspire even greater awe of the Creator.[3] For him science is a form of worship, and this leads naturally to investigations across many disciplines to learn about COVID-19 and bring it under human control. This is an important part of the Christian response to the pandemic and complements our prayers for God's intervention and for deliverance from fear and a loss of hope.

Pandemics are integral to the world we experience in which human beings are inextricably linked to all of nature. Viruses and bacteria are indispensable parts of our world and our bodies, and their effects are not entirely harmful. Many viruses lurk quietly in the human body, in the lungs, blood, and nerves, and especially inside multitudes of microbes that colonize the gut. It has been estimated that 380 trillion viruses live on and in our bodies, about ten times the number of bacteria. While some viruses cause illnesses, others coexist with our bodies, and contribute to a superorganism of cohabiting cells, bacteria, fungi and viruses.[4] Acknowledging data like these places viral infections in a new light and directs our attention away from an "us versus them" scenario in which human beings are viewed as being over against the world of nature and God is seen as protecting human beings from the ravages of a hostile natural world.

In this sense, COVID-19 is not a foreign virus but is endemic to our common nature as human beings. Things go wrong because we are human, and this is the world over which God has ultimate control. Natural disasters occur repeatedly, and the death toll can be catastrophic from the likes of earthquakes, tsunamis, and volcanos, but millions also die each year from starvation and infections that are capable of being eradicated. The magnitude of the death toll generally depends upon misguided human decision-making, political ineptitude, and social inequality. In other words, the tragedies are so often made worse by human agency—selfishness, injustice, and overlooking the needs of the poor and vulnerable. This in no way denigrates the belief that God cares deeply for the world with all its suffering and angst.

The challenge for Christians is to be active in seeking to demonstrate that we live in a world marked by stability and order where even a virus is

---

3. Collins, "Science Is a 'Glimpse of God's Mind.'"
4. Pride, "Viruses Can Help Us as Well as Harm Us."

a creation of remarkable complexity that shows forth God's handiwork. In 2020, in the absence of vaccines, public health measures were the best protection against a novel and unknown virus that was proving spectacularly destructive. But even these measures reflected God-given capacities and knowledge that should have been welcomed by people of faith, no matter how limiting and frustrating they undoubtedly were. In 2020 the challenge was to find a balance between the assurance that God was in control and human responsibility to determine how best to overcome the worst effects of a pandemic for which we did not at that time have an assured way of preventing its spread.

In doing this, we were and continue to be guided by Christ's overriding commandment to love God with all our being—heart, soul, mind, and strength, and to love our neighbor as ourselves (Mark 12:29–30). The end result are altruistic actions aimed at helping others as an outworking of our commitment to serve others as those loved by God. This means laying aside fear and anxiety, knowing that, ultimately, God is in control. This is when belief becomes real, as our anxieties are replaced with an intimation of joy and serenity even in the midst of substantial uncertainty, in part because we recognize that the creation groans as it awaits Christ's coming (Rom 8:18–25). Alongside these words of assurance and hope is the realization that human beings like us have been given responsibility for directing and running our world. This may sound grandiose and even arrogant, and yet it is no more than a reflection of our creation in God's image, and it is this that gives us the responsibility of responding to viral outbreaks and resulting diseases. The impetus to acting in these ways is the protection and welfare of the community, our neighbors, and those we are in a position to help and protect. Dependence upon God is never a call to fatalistic quiescence but to responsible selfless action.

Year 1 Lockdown and Plagues of the Past

COVID-19 is not unique in the annals of plagues, even though modern people may think otherwise, since only those in a small number of Asian countries have been exposed to a pandemic.[5] Of the many illustrations available, the one that stands out from a Christian perspective is that of Martin Luther, who was confronted by a plague in his home town of Wittenberg in Germany in 1527. He remained in Wittenberg since he saw it

5. For more details, see my article: "A Pandemic, Science and Faith."

as his pastoral responsibility to minister to the sick and fearful. Although many others were fleeing to relative safety, he and his pregnant wife opened their home for the sick in an attempt to support the ill and dying.

Perhaps unsurprisingly, Luther was criticized for staying and risking the lives of himself and his family. Surely he should have saved himself so that he could continue with his work once the plague had passed. In response, he wrote his now well-known letter, "Whether One May Flee the Plague."[6] In this he explained the importance of caring for one's neighbor, for the community, and taking the necessary steps to protect others. He did not think it was necessarily wrong to flee from death, but that was never to be one's main motivation. He was convinced that we are obliged to assist and help others in the same way as we ourselves would appreciate being helped. Luther was nothing else if not practical, and he urged people to take medicine, to disinfect their homes, and, if at all possible, to avoid people and places in an effort to confine the disease. He also recognized the benefits of hospitals to care for the sick. For Luther, serving God leads to serving one's neighbor, even in the face of terrifying dangers. He argued that a good shepherd, in particular a pastor or church leader, must be prepared to lay down his life for his sheep, following the example of Jesus, the good shepherd. In the absence of the epidemiological and public health knowledge available to us today, Luther's response was all the more remarkable. His straightforward and matter-of-fact responses demonstrate that one can get a long way using common sense and the knowledge that followers of Christ are bound together in Christ's body and so have duties towards their neighbors. This in no way underestimates the importance of scientific input that, incidentally, parallels biblical imperatives; the two align remarkably well in the face of an out-of-control adversary.

Another historic example is provided by the village of Eyam in Derbyshire in England. During the bubonic plague outbreak of 1665–66, the inhabitants of Eyam quarantined themselves to prevent the spread of the plague from their village into the surrounding areas with much larger towns. The source of the plague was cloth coming into the village from London, where the plague was rife. Confronted by mounting deaths, the village's newly arrived priest, William Mompesson, convinced villagers that the right thing to do was quarantine the village rather than spread the plague. He knew that the result was likely to be a high death rate among the villagers, and that eventuated. By the end of the outbreak, more than

---

6. Luther, "Whether One May Flee the Plague."

a quarter of the village's population of almost one thousand had died. The plague, however, was contained. The village had discovered the policy of "social distancing," something that required not just isolation from the surrounding population but also open-air funeral services to reduced physical proximity and families burying their own dead in fields and gardens rather than the village graveyard.[7]

As we look back at these examples of Christian leaders four to five hundred years ago, what shines through is the strength of their faith in Christ, a hope that extended beyond this life, and their commitment to helping those around them, giving comfort and sustenance whenever and wherever possible. They appear to have accepted the situation in which they found themselves; in all probability they had no option, since they knew nothing else. Their pragmatism, though, is to be applauded, since it shunned extremes: on the one hand, they did not suggest that they sit back and trust the Lord regardless of how they acted, but neither did they advocate self-protection at all costs. They recognized that their and other people's earthly lives were of value, but they also recognized that they were not of ultimate value. They were not to be thrown away needlessly, but neither were they to be wrapped in cotton wool and protected at all costs. Doing good for others, particularly the vulnerable and weak, involved risk, a risk that was worth taking. Ultimately, the value of our lives has an eternal dimension, stemming from the mind of God, our creator and redeemer. This is an ethical perspective it is all too easy to miss in the face of fear or scientific achievements.

Luther and those like him were disadvantaged by the absence of medical advice, but this made decision-making more straightforward. By contrast, we have options: to ignore medical advice, do the opposite and listen exclusively to medical advice, or seek a balance between the two on the ground that the best medical advice reveals God's provision for his creation. In other words, Christians are to appreciate the role of medical science and in doing so be thankful for the science that lies behind it. This is the hand of God at work in a fallen world. God's purposes on the one hand and epidemiology and public health advice on the other complement each other.

The vulnerability of European and other societies in the sixteenth to twentieth centuries is obvious to us today, but our own vulnerability is hidden by our scientific achievements in controlling so many facets of disease,

---

7. Masson, "Why Is Eyam Significant?"

especially infectious diseases. We have forgotten how vulnerable we are and are tempted to go to the other extreme and act as though we are indestructible. All too readily we come to regard ourselves as omnipotent, leading us into the devastating trap of downplaying our mortality. We are, of course, deeply troubled by cancer, especially in a young person, but this is viewed as an aberration to our ongoing invincibility. It is an insult and should not happen, made all the worse by the absence of a drug to vanquish it. There are even some who venture to propose that death can be conquered by technology; one of the travesties of our condition, they argue, is aging and its end-point of death, even when this is the death of centenarians. It is against this background that we have to view COVID-19 and its unwelcome and unacceptable intrusion. It forces us to recognize the physicality of our existence, the vulnerability of our bodies, and our coexistence with viruses and bacteria.

A pandemic underlines the fragility of our lives and of the world as a whole. This is hardly novel, of course, since viral infections are far from being the first example of this; the possibility of nuclear obliteration is an obvious example that has been present for over seventy years. And yet there are differences. With viruses we do not know who is being infected nor whether we may be inadvertently infecting others. This leads to fear and suspicion and emphasizes the deep insecurity of our lives. Our pretension to control the world has been shattered. The result is fear, the type of fear that destroys our dreams and hopes and takes us away from God. It diminishes us and leads to self-preservation rather than a willingness to open ourselves to being prepared to sacrifice our comforts, and even lose our lives, for the sake of our neighbors (John 15:13). It ignores a basic injunction that we are to be strong and courageous, and not fear, knowing that the Lord our God will never forsake us (Deut 31:6).

It is no wonder that whole societies are terrified by a virus about which initially we knew very little, and that, until the appearance of vaccines, ruled our lives and hopes in ways with which we were unaccustomed. But not only does this apply to whole societies; it also applies to Western Christians for whom dominion over nature has become what is always expected. We have become so used to controlling the natural world that when that control fails we feel let down. The temptation is to think we have been let down by God, and yet up to now we have been blessed because our God-bestowed human creativity in exploring the world and developing means of controlling it has benefited us through the development of vaccines, antibiotics, and numerous other agents. We overlook the fact that God has been at work in and through medical technology and the numerous blessings flowing from this. Not only this, God continues to be at work, as laboratories galore throughout the world worked feverishly to define the genetic characteristics of this particular virus, emerging with a surprisingly wide range of safe and effective vaccines.

The Role of Public Health Scientists

Abiding by public health measures is a crucial way of protecting others as well as ourselves and is an outcome of love for one's neighbor. These points were amply demonstrated by the success of lockdown measures in New Zealand in 2020.[8] At the time I argued that the standout messages were the prominent role played by science in undergirding political decision-making, decisive and empathic leadership, and the subsequent high level of trust placed by the community in the political decision-makers. The willingness of political leaders to listen to scientific advice and enter into dialogue with public health specialists and epidemiologists stood out as exemplary. The two dominant messages coming from the political leadership at the height of the pandemic at that time were: "be kind," and the notion of being a "team of five million" (the population of New Zealand). These highlighted the importance of community, the interests of one's neighbors, and the need to treat each other with kindness and consideration. While these were not put forward as Christian standards, they bore striking resemblance to the Christian values of neighborly love, living for each other, putting the interests of others before one's own interests, and demonstrating the gifts of the Spirit. It was these that enabled the country to live through an early very harsh lockdown aimed at "eliminating" the virus from the population.

While the situation had changed by 2021 and 2022 with the arrival of vaccines and vaccine mandates, and while the more recent practices have in my view failed to uphold Christian values, the 2020 lockdown experience was exemplary. It mirrored Jesus's well-known teaching on love for one's neighbor as strikingly exemplified by his parable of the Good Samaritan (Luke 10:25–37). In simple terms, we are to look beyond ourselves and our own individualistic interests. Like the Samaritan, the New Zealand response

---

8. I covered this territory in my 2021 article: "A Christian Perspective on New Zealand's Response to COVID-19," 67–78.

was that of an alien government, that is, largely secular, determined to rescue its citizens and protect them from an unknown level of harm.

The wellbeing of the community is to be our first priority; we are to do everything possible to protect our neighbors from the vicissitudes of a rampant viral infection, a task that falls to everyone, since all are members of the community. In Christian terms, we are all members of the one body, so exquisitely demonstrated by the church as the body of Christ. If one suffers all parts suffer, and if one part is honored all parts benefit. Not only this, but different parts of the body have a diversity of gifts and abilities, including leadership and healing. Hence, the role of a range of experts, all of whom are to be included in contributing to discussions about the best way forward.

For Christians, COVID-19 demonstrates that science has to be taken seriously. The biblical writers in isolation cannot provide a direct answer that will alleviate the social and health dilemmas surrounding us, but they are core in helping Christians face up to the fear and uncertainty brought about by a viral pandemic. However, physical healing depends upon medical-scientific contributions, from highly skilled staff in intensive care units, subsequent rehabilitation, and potentially, the widespread availability of an effective vaccine. Science and Scripture work in tandem, and within a Christian environment, both are to be treated with the utmost seriousness. It is never a question of either/or.

Human Beings, the Natural World, and Pandemics

The temptation to ask why raises its unhelpful head repeatedly during a pandemic, as though it is any different from an "epidemic" of breast cancer, dysentery, measles, malnutrition, or dementia. Of course, there are major medical differences between these varying conditions, and yet all in their assorted ways cause suffering, early death, and a host of lost opportunities. Far more effective and, I would argue, far more appropriate for Christians are scientific ways forward in the form of basic genetic analyses, epidemiological modeling, and public health priorities. These are all God-given directions, and we ignore them at our peril. Francis Collins, as previously mentioned, regards science as a form of worship, and this in turn demands that we take science seriously and strive to utilize it for the betterment of our neighbors and of the communities in which we live. As we function in this manner, we begin to realize the complementary nature of science and faith. This is a far cry from the antagonism that some claim exists between the two.

In view of the history of epidemics and pandemics, the COVID-19 pandemic, or something along those lines, should have been expected. Tragically, with a very small number of exceptions, countries failed to benefit from the lessons of earlier manifestations of rampant viral infections. Well recognized contributory factors, including the dangers of wildlife markets in heavily populated countries, with their facility of transferring animal viruses to the human population, were overlooked, while self-isolation, the critical importance of social/physical isolation, and contact tracing were frequently downplayed. These are responsibilities given to humans by God, and their neglect is nothing less than a manifestation of foolhardiness, as other activities and interests are given greater priority than human health and wellbeing.

The problem lies in humans' proclivity to self-interest. This manifests itself when politicians put such priorities aside with their urge to be re-elected. Similarly when business interests do the same with their desire to protect their bottom lines and the wellbeing of their shareholders. Even individuals, with their longing for freedom and self-expression, are to blame. The end result is that nothing is done to prepare adequately for pandemics until the situation becomes so dire that drastic measures have to be implemented even when they override all normal expectations. This is a pessimistic conclusion but is justified for as long as people and societies fail to acknowledge that God has the whole world in his hands. Christians assert that everything that lives and moves has its being in him, so that when we pray, we are speaking to a personal God who holds the universe as a whole and each of its component parts together in love (Col 1:17). This realization lies at the heart of Christian faith with its dependence upon the sovereign work of God in Jesus Christ and its determination to bring under control natural forces with the potential to overwhelm us and all we hold dear. Christians have a responsibility to all those around them, as outlined so perceptively in Jeremiah: "Seek the welfare of the city where I have sent you into exile, and pray to the Lord on its behalf, for in its welfare you will find your welfare" (Jer 29:7). They are an integral part of the society in which they live.

Epidemics and pandemics are integral to the world we experience, and human beings are inextricably linked to all of nature. Things go wrong because we are human and because we make mistakes and poor judgments; but this is still the world over which God has ultimate control. Natural disasters occur repeatedly. On some occasions the death toll is magnified by a lack of resources to combat it, by the poor quality of medical and political decision-making, and by the inequality that characterizes most societies.

Christians are to be active in seeking to model social fairness within a world marked by stability and order. There is much we do not understand—theologically, socially, and scientifically. Nevertheless, human beings have considerable abilities capable of unlocking the secrets of the world in which they live, including the structure of viruses, how they function, and why they cause so much damage to human beings. These are gifts from God and should be welcomed and utilized by people of faith, who have confidence that God is leading them as they explore and dissect this small area within God's magnificent universe. Christians who are scientists can be encouraged by the message to Isaiah that "those who wait for the Lord shall renew their strength, they shall mount up with wings like eagles, they shall run and not be weary, they shall walk and not faint" (Is 40:31).

The core message is that we are to find a balance between the assurance that God is in control, and the importance of human responsibility in determining how best to overcome the worst effects of a pandemic. Loving God with every facet of our being, utilizing all the gifts at our disposal, and loving our neighbor as ourselves (Mark 12:29–30) are fundamental prerequisites for Christians. As we serve others, we learn to lay aside fear and anxiety, knowing that ultimate control lies in God's hands. This enables us to experience just a hint of joy and peace even in the midst of substantial uncertainty, knowing as we do that the creation groans as it awaits Christ's coming (Rom 8:18–25). Public health measures are a crucial means of protecting others and making real love for one's neighbor.

Science in the Service of God

Those in the West have become so accustomed to being able to exert control over illness that we resent being confronted by an illness over which we have no meaningful control. Lyman Stone has commented: "The modern world has suddenly become reacquainted with the oldest traveling companion of human history: existential dread and the fear of unavailable, inscrutable death."[9] In his view, we will not be saved by a vaccine or antibiotic simply because we are ill-equipped psychologically and culturally to cope with a marauding pandemic. This may be an excessively pessimistic conclusion, but it serves to bring home to us that we find it exceedingly difficult

9. Stone, "Christianity has been Handling Epidemics for 2000 Years."

to accept that we do not have total control over our lives. This should not come as a surprise, since all of us have to face pain and suffering at some point in our lives, as well as in the lives of those close to us, and yet we tend to think of these as aberrant intrusions into a disease-free existence. We overestimate the power of medical science to overcome illness and distress.

Confronted by a seemingly out-of-control pandemic reminds us that we are no longer twenty first century people but more akin to fourteenth-century people. For us the Black Death was a historic pandemic in an almost forgotten world, far removed from our technologically sophisticated civilization. We spend our time planning for ever-increasing lifespans and improvements in the quality of health of whole communities, not for salvaging communities decimated by a virus for which there was for a long time no vaccine. The past appears to have caught up with the present, and in doing so holds out the prospect of devastating it. Our response is to say that this is not the way things should be; science has failed, and Christians are left as bewildered as everyone else.

This is because we have become entranced by our love of technology, including medical technology. Christians have to ask themselves whether they are depending upon God or upon a technological fix, in the form of a drug to lower blood pressure, or an antidepressant, or plastic surgery to correct a congenital defect. There is nothing inherently amiss with any of these, but are they essential, and what implications might they have for our thinking and attitudes? It is urgent that Christians of all persuasions seek to balance the benefits and drawbacks of science and technology in contemporary life, rejoicing in that which enhances appreciation of the goodness of God and cultivating awareness of the limits of that same technology. These limits include the ever-present possibility that technological delights have become idols that have subtly replaced dependence upon our creator and redeemer. Until recently, thoughts along these lines would have sounded unduly theoretical and pessimistic, but that is no longer the case as an out-of-control virus hit whole populations with terrifying force prior to the appearance of effective vaccines.

This has been surprisingly evident in this pandemic because some of the most technologically advanced countries have been most severely affected. This is counter-intuitive and not what one would have expected in pre-pandemic times. The reasons for this are undoubtedly legion but include explicit or implicit rejection of scientific advice. And if, as I have been arguing, the advice to quarantine, contact trace, and genetically test reflect God's good way of responding to a pandemic, rejection of this advice is nothing less than human beings placing themselves over God. It reflects arrogance and an idolizing of human priorities, an unexpected conclusion when what is being rejected is scientific advice.

These thoughts were strikingly brought home to me when going through the page proofs of an article of mine on transhumanism, written before the onset of the COVID-19 pandemic. I had given it the title: "The Transhumanist Vision: Technological Bliss or Tragic Misadventure?"[10] To the uninitiated, anything to do with transhumanism sounds exotic and highly unrealistic. At its most basic it tends to revolve around a new way of thinking that starts from the premise that the human condition is open to being altered in dramatic new ways. These include the development of super-intelligent machines, personality pills, space colonization, molecular nanotechnology, vastly extended lifespans, uploading of our consciousness into a virtual reality, and reanimation of cryonics (deep frozen) patients. This is the picture of triumphant technology leading the human race into a glorious future of unalloyed bliss, and liberated from the mysteries and constraints of traditional religion.

Fascinating and even compelling as some of these ideas may be, they ignore the ravages that have been caused by infectious diseases throughout human history, let alone in the twentieth and twenty-first centuries. They also ignore the contribution made by public health measures over the last few centuries, including the central role played by vaccination. True, vaccination has a technological base, but it is all too readily downplayed when compared with regenerative medicine and gene therapy. Perhaps the grand pretensions of the transhumanists are no more than misguided wishful thinking, especially when used as the basis of a secular worldview.

Responding to Scientific Advances

The COVID-19 pandemic has brought to the fore the tension between a population's health and its economic interests. Although the two frequently go hand-in-hand, this is not always the case. On occasion, the two may move in diametrically opposite directions. What is good for the one is not always good for the other. This is a balancing act one meets repeatedly in other areas, such as in science, when that which is ideal from a scientific angle may be far from ideal ethically. Some scientific activities should not be

10. Jones, "The Transhumanist Vision," 95–108.

carried out because of their negative ethical repercussions. Consequently, a society driven largely by economic interests will have difficulty in coming to terms with the stringent health requirements in a COVID-19 situation where the aim is to save lives, especially those of vulnerable members of society. This requires an appreciation of values other than economic ones.

The model adopted by a small isolated country like New Zealand highlights these tensions (see *The Role of Public Health Scientists*, 48–49). This model led to the saving of thousands of lives, an important public health measure, that also makes a theological point. The saving of lives is to be welcomed by Christians as a mark of God's blessing in the sense that it is a manifestation of the work of those who are using their expertise for the benefit of all. They are using abilities bestowed upon them by God and are being used, explicitly or not, in his service.

A situation akin to that of COVID-19 reminds those of us living in the affluent parts of the world that we are generally privileged and protected. Most of the population does not routinely have to worry about imminent death, apart from accidents, suicide, war, and some congenital conditions. This is not the case in the majority world, where starvation, common and readily treated infections, diarrhea, and other eminently curable conditions are rife and kill numerous people, mainly children. An out-of-control COVID-19 reveals what life is like for the majority of our fellow humans. And that is a salutary experience. It also places on the privileged a burden to assist the disadvantaged.

For Christians, COVID-19 demonstrates that science has to be taken seriously. The biblical writers cannot provide an answer that, on its own, will alleviate the social and health dilemmas surrounding us. They are crucial in helping Christians face up to the fear and uncertainty brought about by the pandemic; this is what I look for from Christian leaders. However, physical healing will come from scientific investigations; namely, producing an effective vaccine and making it widely available, and, in the meantime, public health remedies that will alleviate the worst effects of the infection. Physical well-being, while not everything, has enormous repercussions for overall health, including spiritual health.

Christians in the West need to take seriously Jesus's comment in response to being asked about those who had been slaughtered by Pilate in the temple. He was categorical: they were not worse sinners than others (Luke 13:1–5). Similarly, those killed when the tower in Siloam fell on them were innocent. For Jesus the challenge was not to discover where God was in these tragedies, but to repent and seek God's mercy and follow him. This is less spectacular than one that claims to see God's hand in response to people's faith or sin. But that does not appear to be the way in which God works.

Theologian Tom Wright points out that in Acts 11:27–30 when there was going to be a great famine the disciples asked three questions: Who is going to be at special risk when this happens? What can we do to help? And who shall we send? Wright comments: "Some might look at this and think, Well, that's pretty untheological as a response. It's just pragmatic. But that would actually be the really 'untheological' response. Here we stumble upon one of the great principles of the kingdom of God—the principle that God's kingdom, inaugurated through Jesus, is all about restoring creation the way it was meant to be. God always wanted to work in his world through loyal human beings. That is part of the point of being made 'in God's image.'"[11] God was going to work through them.

In building on this, Wright is more specific, with his assertion that God has delegated the running of many aspects of the world to human beings—authority has been delegated to his image-bearers. From this it follows that "we need proper investigation and accountability for whatever it was that caused the virus to leak out and for the lesser ways in which various countries and governments have, or have not, dealt wisely in preparing for a pandemic and then handling it when it rushed upon us."[12]

This is where science enters the picture; it is God's image-bearers doing the work for which they have been trained. It is God's work even when undertaken by those who do not recognize God's involvement in the world and in science. This is to take God seriously, as it is to take human responsibility (and irresponsibility) seriously. No matter how unspiritual this sounds, it comes to grips with God's sovereignty and human beings acting as God's representatives. This is what Christians have been called to do, having been given the gifts and resources enabling us to act in these ways. At their best, the Christian faith and scientific investigations walk hand-in-hand to the mutual benefit of both and the world.

Science and the Christian Community

A viral pandemic is unusual, and yet fears have beset the church on many occasions over the years. In 1948 C. S. Lewis was confronted by the

11. Wright, *God and the Pandemic*, 25.
12. Wright, *God and the Pandemic*, 43.

widespread fears generated by the coming of the atomic bomb.[13] This led to his writing an essay that encapsulated his thinking at the time: "On Living in an Atomic Age." His sagacity and common sense shine through.

For Lewis, people were to live under the shadow of the atomic bomb as they previously lived when plague was rampant or when Viking raiders could have cut their throats. He also reminded them that they already lived with cancer, syphilis, air raids, railway accidents, and accidents on the roads. The commonplaceness of these examples makes us sit up and take notice. They bring us down to earth and force us to face up to the normality of danger. We have lived with it all our lives, even though we have come to terms with so much that could end our lives at any moment. The challenge is to think about this and ask how we cope with imminent dangers.

This is the point C. S. Lewis was making all those years ago. He did not want people to exaggerate the novelty of the impending danger even though it appeared so much more pressing and cataclysmic than anything in recent memory. He simply wanted them to pull themselves together, a response that on the surface appeared as unspiritual as Tom Wright's response to the pandemic. Lewis reminded people that if they were going to be destroyed by an atomic bomb, they should get on and do the ordinary things of life—working, praying, listening to music, chatting to friends. He did not want them to act like frightened sheep, and he definitely did not want their minds to be dominated by fear.[14]

Christians are to get on with living, even in the midst of overbearing circumstances. My contention in this chapter has been that we recognize the contribution of scientists as an integral part of God's providence. Every scientific achievement and development is not to be welcomed, since scientists are flaw-ridden, like the rest of humankind. Nevertheless, in general terms, Christians are to learn to wonder at the achievements of medical science even as they temper some of the more extravagant claims of some scientists.

The challenge is to balance a range of opposing narratives. Some degree of control over a pandemic can be achieved by public health measures and ongoing scientific inquiries. These are to be seen as God at work in controlling nature and are integral to his provisions for humankind. As such, they are appropriate matters for prayer as God's people seek God's direction and guidance. Science and faith are vital partners in sketching a

---

13. Lewis, "On Living in an Atomic Age," 115.
14. Lewis, "On Living in an Atomic Age," 115–16.

way forward, not in some outlandish attempt to inappropriately exercise control over nature, but in seeking ways in which faults in natural processes can be healed and a return to wholeness brought about.

But as has emerged very clearly, science's contribution was not limited to public health and epidemiology measures. Vaccines were produced in startlingly rapid time, a further reflection on the goodness of God along with the application of the creative intent of numerous scientists. As we shall see in the next chapter, they have brought light and hope in the face of a catastrophic pandemic, but equally they have raised a plethora of novel issues, some of which have proved immensely contentious.

4

Vaccines, Vaccine Mandates, Freedom, and Love of Neighbor

Year 2: Vaccines and Vaccine Mandates

IN THE PREVIOUS CHAPTER my aim was to emphasize the role played by science and scientists in responding to the first stages of the pandemic—lockdown—and the part played by public health specialists. At the time separating people from each other was the most that was available. However, even then it was widely recognized that the ultimate remedy lay in effective vaccination, although it was widely doubted that this could be accomplished in a few months or even a year. This was a reasonable doubt, since the development of new vaccines generally spans a number of years. But never before in recent memory has there been a pandemic on the scale of COVID-19, and so the resources that poured into it worldwide were unprecedented. And the unlikely became reality; effective and safe vaccines started to appear in the early part of 2021. Focus now moved to ending the pandemic through vaccine distribution.

Initially, hundreds of vaccine candidates emerged as contenders as research was conducted in numerous countries, with three initially emerging as dominant players—Pfizer/BioNTech, Moderna, and Oxford University/AstraZeneca. Regardless of the teething problems and concerns around various side-effects associated with some of the vaccines, this was indisputably a massive scientific achievement, no less than a gift from God to be used for the benefit of his creation. This has been most prominently and forcefully pointed out repeatedly by Francis Collins from his perspective as a vocal Christian and leading biomedical scientist. And yet, all was not well.

Surprisingly, the remedy many of us looked forward to and rejoiced in when vaccines were produced in an amazingly short timeframe turned out to be a source of deep division and unyielding hostility. And even more surprising, this response has come from, among others, Christians, especially those on the conservative wings of church communities. Fracture lines began to appear and relationships started to unravel when church communities were faced with division in their ranks over an issue that few would have predicted pre-pandemic. Decisions over mandating vaccination by governments as well as a range of professions and organizations, including churches, have proven unnervingly schismatic and troubling. And in some quarters this resistance has been given a theological slant.

Many things have been learned by living through a pandemic, and one of them is that the move from lockdown to vaccination marks a significant transition between two stages: from quiescence to action. Each has its tensions and each is associated with challenges for everyone, including Christians and the church. Lockdowns are imposed by the government or government agencies; the use of vaccines is an individual decision, and even when mandated by the government the onus is placed on individuals to respond, possibly under duress. From a Christian angle, this second stage has proved to be far more demanding, since it requires far more thought on the part of Christian leadership to know how to respond and what advice to give ordinary Christians. It forces those in authority to search the Scriptures and uncover the values and principles used in the early church and apply them to the contemporary context.

Year 2 (2021) proved a maelstrom of misinformation, animosity, and confusion within some Christian circles. I doubt there were many people pre-2021 who had predicted that this would be the case. Perhaps we should not have been as surprised as most of us were, because for over two hundred years there have been resolute anti-vaxxers, who have also tended to be proponents of alternative medicines. But what emerged in 2021 and beyond extends far beyond these, and this is probably due to a mix of social-political forces, aided and abetted in Christian circles by a raft of theological emphases.

At the Margins

Tracing Historical Paths

The practice of inoculation by variolation emerged as a means of dealing with smallpox in the eighteenth century. This approach, though, was attacked by some as an affront to God's will on the ground that only God should determine the natural order of who is to be exposed to smallpox.[1] On the other hand, variolation had its Christian advocates, such as Cotton Mather, a leading American clergyman in the early eighteenth century. In spite of opposition, inoculation by variolation, using smallpox material as the basis for the vaccine, continued to grow throughout the eighteenth century, leading to the epochal studies of Edward Jenner in 1796. In these he demonstrated immunity to smallpox by using cowpox material for arm-to-arm inoculation rather than exposing children to smallpox itself. From that time on, vaccination against smallpox has spread, until systematic implementation of mass smallpox immunization culminated in what was widely considered to be its global eradication in 1979.

Stunning as these scientific developments were, there has been a constant low level of resistance to vaccination, suggesting that resistance to COVID-19 vaccination is far from a novel phenomenon. Since the end of the eighteenth century excitement at the emergence of medically proven vaccines has been repeatedly paralleled by outbreaks of misinformation and resistance to one vaccine after another. In Jenner's time the idea of injecting someone with a cowpox blister as protection against smallpox raised a host of sanitary, religious, and political objections. Satirists had a field day with their depictions of people spouting cow horns, a fear with roots in religious and cultural stigma surrounding the pollution of blood with animal matter. A contemporary cartoon showed Jenner feeding children to a "vaccination monster" on the ground that he benefited financially from this dubious exercise.

Anti-vaccine pamphlets in opposition to Jenner's work predicted catastrophe, with the vaccinated ending up deformed and gangrenous. These beliefs were more pronounced among the poor and the working classes who did not trust governments and objected to compulsory vaccination. Anti-vaccination campaigns sprung up in the United Kingdom during the Victorian era on the ground that it was a dangerous procedure being thrust upon society's most vulnerable children. For some it was nothing less than medical despotism. The outcome was that vaccination against smallpox was resisted for many years, with the result that smallpox outbreaks continued

---

1. Harris, "Rash Decisions."

for a hundred years in a number of countries.[2] In 1904, thirty people died in rioting in Rio de Janeiro, while in Europe mass anti-vaccination movements were common. It took a later epidemic in 1908 to lead to general acceptance of smallpox vaccination.

Throughout these years, vaccination was mandated in the United Kingdom; for instance, in 1853, it was mandated that infants had to be vaccinated by four months of age. In response to increasing mortality rates, further legislation followed in 1867 leading to increases in punishment for failure to vaccinate children. Compulsory vaccination was resisted in both the United Kingdom and United States in the nineteenth century, with anti-vaccination movements basing their stance on the loss of civil liberty and government overreach.[3] Nineteenth-century anti-vaccination organizations questioned the ethics of vaccination and its safety, leading eventually to some drawback on the penalties for vaccine refusal.

Following this success with smallpox, vaccines have proved successful in controlling countless infectious diseases from cholera, rabies, and typhoid through to tuberculosis, diphtheria, and polio, and on to measles, mumps, and shingles, plus many more. Polio epidemics followed, but even when effective vaccines became available in the mid-1950s, there were pockets of resistance accompanied by outlandish claims and misinformation, originating in ethical and theological debates, government overreach, and a skepticism of science.[4]

Mandates to ensure high levels of vaccination have an uneasy history. The argument that vaccines serve the greater good has been resolutely advocated, especially when mandating that immunization is required for children to attend public schools. By the same token, they have been as resolutely resisted on a host of grounds, including those of religious and civil liberty. Over the past twenty years or so, skepticism of the science behind vaccinations has emerged and subsequently grown, reaching a zenith in 1998 with the claims of Andrew Wakefield that the MMR (measles, mumps, rubella) vaccine is linked to autism. The fragile basis of this claim and subsequent evidence demonstrating its basis in outright scientific fraud[5] has done little to dispel the anti-vaccination furor that has taken on a life of its own. This illustrates a central feature of the debate on vaccines and

2. Parsons, "Vaccine Resistance Is Not New."
3. Harris, "Rash Decisions."
4. Parsons, "Vaccine Resistance Is Not New."
5. Deer, *The Doctor Who Fooled the World*.

mandates: negativity about vaccines extends far beyond science and scientific data, and is a complex socio-cultural phenomenon that has proved resistant to scientific data and arguments alone.

Scientific Excellence and the Emergence of Vaccines

The way in which COVID-19 vaccines have been produced since early 2020 has been truly astounding. The achievement of producing new vaccines in a year has exceeded the wildest expectations of even virologists. This is science at its most spectacular, and Christians should rejoice at what has been accomplished. It is not too outlandish to recognize this as an answer to prayer and to the highest abilities of human beings acting as God's vice-regents. We should stand back in awe and rejoice in some of the highest achievements of those created in the image of God, who as the psalmist puts it are "made a little lower than the angels . . . to rule over the works of your hands; you have put everything under their feet" (Ps 8:5–6).

Over recent centuries whole societies have been transformed by vaccines as devastating infections have been either brought under control or practically eliminated. They have led to dramatic increases in life expectancy and decreases in neonatal and childhood mortality. As a result of these developments, the notion of what constitutes good health has been transformed. While this revolution has been brought about by the application of science, it has equally demonstrated the goodness of God exhibited through the creativity of humans made in his image and utilizing this creativity to overcome evil and premature death. This has been an extension of the manner in which the Christian church historically established hospitals and sought to provide medical and nursing care where desperately needed.

There has regularly been tension between collective responsibility and the individual's freedom of choice about what in their view is best for their own bodies. This tension is aggravated when there are hints that vaccines may damage the individual, specifically a child. As touched on above, a poignant illustration of this was Andrew Wakefield's condemnation of the MMR vaccine on account of its alleged association with autism in children. The consequences have been cataclysmic, with significant declines in vaccination rates in many countries, the re-emergence of measles as a serious childhood illness, and the bolstering of the anti-vaccine movement.

While not unexpected, opposition to COVID-19 vaccines has been bolstered by conspiracy theories, with their misinformation, disinformation, and rampant deception. The opposition coming from Christian organizations has given the impression that there are biblical grounds for it, since it has emanated mainly from those in the conservative wing of the church (see *The Perceived Threat Posed by Vaccine Mandates*, 64–66).

The virus, SARS-CoV-2, has caused a massive number of deaths worldwide and left many more ill. To date well over five hundred million people have been diagnosed with COVID-19, with over six million deaths (and this is probably an underestimate by a factor of three to five). The appalling catastrophes in a number of countries are a stark reminder that the virus can do untold damage to the health and welfare of any society. While infection is asymptomatic or mild in most people (85 percent), the remaining 15 percent develop severe disease, with many requiring admissions to an intensive care unit. Long COVID, with persistent symptoms and reduced quality of life, occurs in more than 40 percent of patients who have apparently recovered from COVID-19. This is an increasingly serious problem affecting well over one hundred million people. Vaccination both protects individuals against infection and protects others by reducing the risk of passing the virus on to other people. Unfortunately, these generalizations are just that, since the data are subject to change as new variants emerge, with greater or less degrees of morbidity.

The safety and efficacy of the vaccines have been rigorously assessed, having been tested in animals and then through the three phases of clinical trials in humans. During the human clinical trials, each vaccine has been tested on tens of thousands of volunteers for safety and efficacy. Clinical trials of COVID-19 vaccines were undertaken in different countries where there were high infection rates, enabling the rapid assessment of their efficacy. The phenomenal speed of approval was made possible by governments and research funding agencies committing vast sums of money and people to the enterprise and with considerable global sharing of data.

These vaccines are extremely safe. To date around twelve billion doses of vaccines have been given. Safety continues to be monitored through post-marketing surveillance and safety monitoring systems. The side effects are generally minor, and even the blood clots identified with some of the vaccines are a rare (five in a million doses) adverse effect. Effectiveness varies with the vaccine, but some are up to at least 90 percent effective (Pfizer) in the first few months following two doses. Three doses have become the norm, with four being administered in some countries.

At the Margins

The Perceived Threat Posed by Vaccine Mandates

Mandating that people are vaccinated has taken on a life of its own. I shall touch on opposition stemming from Christian groups.[6] In the United Kingdom a range of Christian church leaders sent an open letter to the prime minister. They regarded vaccine passports as an unethical form of coercion and a violation of the principle of informed consent; in their eyes this would lead to the creation of a two-tier society, a form of "medical apartheid," since it would create an underclass of people who would be excluded from important areas of public life. Even more starkly, they foresaw the end of liberal democracy and the creation of a surveillance state. They categorically rejected the notion that some people were to be deemed as social undesirables by the state since, from their perspective, this would amount to a denial of the truth of the gospel.

Similar opposition to vaccine passports has been evident in Australia with open letters to the prime minister. In one of these, written by three Baptist pastors, the prospect of vaccine passports raised the specter of "therapeutic totalitarianism," with the potential to dehumanize and control citizens on the grounds of personal health and safety. An overriding concern was that the government was coercing people's conscience, especially as in some cases there may be valid reasons for their hesitancy about vaccination. These concerns are not specifically Christian in that they do not have an ostensible Christian basis, although an offshoot of more immediate relevance to churches was the possibility that some people—the unvaccinated—would be refused entry into churches and so would be unable to hear the message of the Christian gospel. This point was brought out in another letter, this time written by a group of Presbyterian and Baptist ministers, with their claim that Christians should never be unable to meet together physically for worship. In their eyes, it is not the place of any government to tell the church it cannot gather to worship.

Views of this nature stem from the belief that Christianity is the natural bedrock of a nation, leading to the stance that these restrictions are nothing less than an encroachment by the state on the authority of the church. This stance is made possible by a libertarian and individualist streak that is novel within Christian thinking. It also opposes the validity of public health measures in the form of lockdowns and vaccination.

---

6. I have dealt with the issues this section in greater detail in Jones, "Religious Concerns about COVID-19."

These are viewed as moral matters, and therefore matters of conscience, and are considered an assault on the Lordship of Christ. In effect, the scientific contribution has been discounted along with commitment to the community and the welfare of those within the community. In responding in this manner, the usual Christian emphasis on love for one's neighbor and protection of the vulnerable and the dispossessed has disappeared. This is a serious loss and represents a major shift in moral evaluation. Either way, there is a serious conflation here between Christian and secular reasoning. These statements are made in the name of the church by leaders within the church, and yet most of what is stated could have been written by those completely outside the church. This is made clear by a lack of reference to Christian credentials, such as belief in grace and mercy rather than judgment and in an overt commitment to equality.

When these latter principles form the bedrock of Christian responses, as they do with many mainline churches, they lead to encouragement for individuals to be vaccinated both for their own sake and for the sake of others. However, vaccine mandates were viewed as more problematic. While endorsing their adoption in principle, there was concern over their excessive use and even misuse, excluding people from activities and places that seriously disadvantaged them with no corresponding benefit to society. A Christian perspective leads to using them as a means of benefiting society as a whole and protecting the vulnerable; the one stipulation is that any use is non-discriminatory.[7] In sketching the issues along these lines, an overriding driver is the attempt to hold in tension the encouragement to be vaccinated with the need to limit the use of vaccine mandates to situations where they can be justified on the basis of clear ethical principles. This is not a simple "yes/no" exercise but one that requires discernment on the part of government and of all institutions within society. The thrust of this stance is that church communities are a home and refuge for all, with vaccine mandates limited to their use in exceptional circumstances. An approach along these lines demands a very nuanced response on the part of numerous individuals and groups within society.

We are still left to address the question of why some Christians have proved so hesitant about vaccines and mandates, if not actively opposing them on occasion. This is a science-faith question, since science and faith appear to be pitted against one another. Two predominant reasons present themselves: distrust of scientists and an emphasis on divine health and

---

7. Church of England, *COVID-19: The Ethics of Vaccine Certification*.

miraculous healing in opposition to routine medical therapy. While neither of these is usually headlined as a major issue, they are in my estimation implicit within the debate. Both reasons lead to the same result: a reluctance to accept the dominant role played by science in combatting the COVID pandemic over against reliance on the power and work of God. This is an outworking of the secular-sacred divide, with each militating against the other. For some, what they regard as excessive reliance upon science to cope with the pandemic leads to a diminution in reliance upon God. In these terms, once the balance is tilted in favor of science, one's faith in God will suffer. Imposing mandates upon those reluctant to be vaccinated is seen as an added threat to Christian witness.

This still does not entirely answer the query of why the biomedical and health sciences are so much more problematic than the physical sciences. For this we probably have to look to the dependence of biology on evolutionary thinking, and this for many conservative Christians is regarded as a stance that casts doubt on the trustworthiness of the Bible. No matter how far removed this is from vaccines, the production of vaccines has been a sterling success for scientific innovation, and that in the eyes of some Christians reinforces the status of science and denigrates the need for God and dependence upon God and his ways of working in the world. Once more we are back at the fragmentation of the vision some have of God's world, a fragmentation I reject as doing grave injustice to his world. I find conclusions along these lines deeply saddening and a misreading of how God works in the world.

Coping with Different Viewpoints in the Church

Although the types of opposition from Christian groups make headlines, it is a deviation from dominant historical Christian patterns of behavior as seen supremely in the work and writings of Francis Collins.[8] His commitment to biomedical science stands out as a guiding light for the church. Historically, he fits within the main strands of Christian witness: demonstrated so clearly in caring for the sick, following the manner in which Christ cared for the sick. There is nothing unusual in expecting the church to play its part in combatting a widespread and contagious virus, as was witnessed with epidemics such as smallpox and the plague. On these

---

8. Francis Collins came to prominence as a Christian with his 2007 book, *The Language of God*.

occasions, efforts were made by leading theologians and church leaders to respond as best they could, using the understanding they had, even when it was at the cost of their own safety and security.

As described in chapter 3, Martin Luther acted in exemplary fashion in the face of the terrors of the plague, doing his best to care for the community and doing all he could to protect those around him. By today's standards he had few resources, but he used what was available to him. We can speculate that had he had vaccines available to him, he would have been the first to advocate their use.

The major thrust of mainline Christian responses is that vaccination protects not only the individual but the individual's community. This immediately redirects the spotlight from the individual onto the community. The core position is, therefore, in favor of vaccination rather than against it. And so, when vaccine mandates are under consideration and freedom to attend church is being debated, the importance of vaccination should never be downplayed. This means that care is required in working out how best to translate biblical passages from the early church into the contemporary Christian world, especially that of very large churches.

The major concern of Christians should be the Lordship of Christ. Are vaccines against COVID (or any other viral infection) a threat to the Lordship of Christ? If they are, this is a legitimate reason for rejecting them as Christians, but it is the only legitimate reason. This is a categorical stance that serves as a bulwark against a host of ephemeral reasons based in secular thinking. In an attempt to find relevant biblical models, I have turned to Paul's reasoning on whether or not those in the early church could eat food offered to idols (1 Cor 8:1–13). This was a highly contentious topic for some of these churches, situated as they were in the midst of societies saturated with idol worship. How were the Christians in these churches to approach this very practical and divisive issue? For Paul, it was not the act of eating food that was central but how their action would be seen by fellow believers. Would it strengthen their faith or be a distraction? Similarly with vaccines. What effect does rejection of vaccination have on the faith of other Christians, especially those with whom you normally worship? Conversely, what will be the effect of being vaccinated on fellow Christians? Those on both sides of the fence have to consider how their actions will influence their fellow believers.

In a public health crisis, there is an added dimension, namely, what effect will my actions have on the health of fellow believers and on the character of the Christian community to which I belong? Does the possibility of chronic ill-health that could be avoided or at the very least ameliorated justify pursuing an ideological goal that is not a core Christian belief? Regardless of our disagreements, we are to demonstrate our love and concern for each other in very practical terms. In a viral pandemic, health concerns are paramount. Will my practice protect or damage the health of my fellow worshippers?

The significance of respecting the consciences of others leads to exercising restraint in inflicting vaccination on them. And yet, this is a policy that works in two ways—both to protect the unvaccinated and just as much to protect the vaccinated. The overarching principle is that the ones to be protected are the vulnerable, both within the church and in the wider community—the elderly, children, the immunocompromised, those with chronic poor health, those unable to protect themselves and living in overcrowded and unhygienic conditions, and those belonging to indigenous communities. These need to be protected more than those who have chosen to remain unvaccinated.

The manner in which a church functions depends, to a large extent, upon government policies and legislation, since these constitute a framework within which the church's decision-making is to take place. The onus is always to be towards protection of the vulnerable and the vaccinated. Inclusion of the vaccinated reflects their decision to act on scientific and health advice to protect both themselves and others as a means of fulfilling their responsibility as Christians. Another way of expressing this is to say that churches should advocate vaccination for those who are part of the church community. Solutions will vary from one situation to another and one country to another, but whatever way forward is determined, it should be based on empathy and respect for each other, and concern for the welfare of all within the church. Best writes: "With care, creativity and a willingness to pursue the good of others ahead of our own convenience and advantage, it should be entirely possible for us to practise *both* our call to minister the gospel to all people *and* our responsibility to love our neighbors and care for the vulnerable, without requiring one of these commitments to trump the other."[9]

The Vatican, having determined that the use of anti-COVID vaccines is morally acceptable, came out in favor of vaccine mandates. All Vatican employees had to show proof of vaccination, a negative test, or had recently recovered from COVID. The pope repeatedly encouraged vaccination and

---

9. Best, "COVID Vaccination and the Church."

referred to vaccines as "an act of love." For him, "Vaccination is a simple but profound way of promoting the common good and caring for each other, especially the most vulnerable."[10] In my estimation this is a remarkable conclusion for a church that is implacably opposed to abortion but has been able to come to terms with the conceptual and practical gap between historic abortions and their purported role in the production of vaccines. It has done this by careful reflection and serious study of the ethical and theological issues at stake.

Years 1 and 2 in Hindsight: The Science-Theology Divide

A major difficulty in the COVID vaccination debate is the apparent inability of those coming from a religious background to distinguish scientific evidence from theological and cultural perspectives. While it is generally unhelpful to regard these two realms as separate watertight compartments, since they constitute a unity, the COVID situation has introduced strange anomalies. Many Christians objecting to COVID vaccines have done so on allegedly scientific grounds, such as the experimental nature of the vaccines and their alleged deleterious side-effects, or on cultural grounds such as the increasing power of governments or the duplicity of government officials and scientists. The theological grounds tend to be far less prominent, except for their postulated link to past abortions. Thankfulness and gratitude to God by the people of God would be a far more fitting response to vaccines than objecting to them on secular grounds.

The role of vaccines in a pandemic brings into sharp focus the science-faith debate that, from my perspective, sometimes tends to be too intellectual and theoretical. Health-related issues bring it into the everyday world and demonstrate the extent to which Christians face up to the integration of the realms so often designated (wrongly in my eyes) as spiritual and secular; they also bring into focus the relationship between church life and the life of the home, work, and play, as well as the trappings of a society's culture.

It is also claimed on occasion that the Bible is the source of all guidance on moral and ethical issues, a claim that I question even as I accept the sufficiency of Scripture to provide a framework for central theological and moral values. It is self-evident that there is no direct biblical teaching on whether anyone should or should not be vaccinated. But there are relevant

---

10. Congregation for the Doctrine of the Faith, "Note on the Morality of Using Some Anti-Covid-19 Vaccines."

principles that apply to all: love of neighbor; service of others; support for widows and orphans—the vulnerable, those unable to fend for themselves, those with compromised immune systems, the elderly, and especially those with chronic health conditions.

From this it follows that when vaccination is discussed, all should be prepared to provide reasons for their position, whether to be vaccinated or not. This is not a private matter, since it impacts everyone else within the community, including the church. Since it is a health matter it has to be of interest to the church as a whole. However, openness has a corollary, and that is the need to respect each other's position, even if regarded as being seriously misguided. A second corollary is that each is to be prepared to give reasons for their stance. All are members of the body of Christ, and judgment belongs to God alone. Not only this, but everyone is flawed, and from time to time all make unwise decisions.

God's Protection

One characteristic of a tense debate such as that of COVID vaccination is the presence of outlandish claims that can only described as misleading—that God will protect us from viruses. There is no evidence for this now, nor has there been in the long history of the human race. The merest glance at the worldwide COVID statistics show that large numbers of Christians, let alone Christian leaders, have died in the pandemic, as they have died in previous pandemics, and also from cancer and heart attacks. A related claim that has emerged is that we should not allow our bodies to be modified by vaccines. Once again, this is hardly a recent phenomenon, since we modify our bodies in numerous ways, by what we eat, how much we do or do not exercise, the therapies and drugs we take to ward off infections and cancers. And those with life-threatening conditions gratefully accept major intrusions into their bodies, such as kidney transplants and the insertion of arterial stents following heart attacks. For Christians, these are evidences of the goodness of God displayed in the creativity and ingenuity of the medical profession. From my perspective, the same can be said of effective vaccines. Thankfulness and gratitude to God by the people of God are a fitting response to vaccines, together with an urgent drive towards their equitable distribution worldwide.

The irony is that the unvaccinated who end up in intensive care or high dependency units will die in the absence of highly technological intrusions into their bodies. They will also endanger the health of the nursing and medical staff looking after them. Love for neighbor is multifaceted.

The lesson to emerge from this is that God protects people through human beings using their God-given expertise. For theologian N. T. Wright, one of the great principles of the kingdom of God is about restoring creation to the way it was meant to be. Consequently, "God always wanted to work in his world through loyal human beings."[11] Hence, in responding to a pandemic, the Christian response is to see what can be done to alleviate the damage being wrought by the virus. There is no hiatus, let alone conflict, between God's purposes in the world and the human response using the best available scientific tools. For Wright, God acts in the world through the poor in Spirit, the meek, the mourners, the peacemakers, and the hungry-for-justice people.

Freedom of Expression and the Church Community

A reason that I, as a Christian, find particularly difficult to accept is the one that places undue emphasis on the importance of freedom of expression, an emphasis that has emerged in some quarters in response to vaccine mandates. The thrust behind this reasoning is that we are to be free to express ourselves as we please, regardless of the needs and hopes of others. However, it takes very little reflection to realize that this longing to be free can only be achieved by restricting, or overlooking, the freedom of others, unless it acknowledges that freedom is a constrained freedom rather than an absolute one. In a pandemic, it has to be seen alongside the responsibility to protect the health and wellbeing of all within the community—both within the church and in wider society. Great care also needs to be taken with claims that the authority of the church is superior to the authority of government.

As in all socio-ethical debates, the freedom of one group has to be weighed against the freedom of another group. This was clearly brought into focus by a rally against vaccine mandates and in favor of freedom for the individual. The hundreds of protesters first interrupted a children's cricket match that had to be cancelled, and then made it very difficult for people to get to shops that had just opened following months of lockdown, seriously interfering with trade and the shopkeepers' livelihood.[12] Their freedom was markedly restricted. This is not a specifically Christian issue,

---

11. Wright, *God and the Pandemic*, 33.
12 Sommerville, "Covid-19: Vaccine Mandate Protesters."

but I would have expected Christians to be acutely aware of the welfare of others beside their own interests and concerns.

In a public health emergency, people cannot act entirely as they wish; they are to act responsibly by public health standards. This is where the authority of the church and the authority of the state interdigitate. Hence, if the church is prepared to allow the non-vaccinated into church services, the non-vaccinated have an obligation to be able to demonstrate that they are not infected, that is, to have negative COVID tests. This is possible with rapid antigen tests. The exact details of how churches operate depend upon myriad factors, from their size and the layout of their buildings and from government regulations to the culture of the church and its adherents.

A fundamental driver of any church or Christian organization is to keep Jesus Christ in the center of all that it is and represents. This is an essential prerequisite, since there are numerous forces with the potential to elevate secondary beliefs into core first-order beliefs. The place of vaccination is a surprisingly destructive one in this regard, even though it can hardly be described as a belief and definitely not a spiritual one. And yet it has divided church communities and whole societies. This should be seen as anathema to Christians, since it is puny and inconsequential when compared with the centerpiece of the gospel, namely, the person and work of Christ. The issues raised by vaccination demand serious dialogue, mutual understanding, and trust, all of which are to be manifest within a church community, and should be facilitated by that community.

In a time of pandemic, no responsible party can ignore determining which course of action will either increase or decrease infection rates. To this end, careful attention should be paid to the scientific expertise of those within one's own society and, if available, within a church community. Why trust those in other countries and on social media, and not those close by and whose integrity has been experienced firsthand?

In the final analysis, church leaders have responsibility for the health and safety and welfare of all within the church building. This is a general principle extending far beyond COVID-19 considerations. There are numerous mandates regarding health and safety, earthquake risks, and fire protection. Why not vaccines with their health consequences?

The Blight of Misinformation

A substantial problem in some Christian communities has been vaccine hesitancy and anti-vaccination sentiments. A number of reasons appear to underlie this phenomenon, including suspicion of scientists and experts including theological experts and the dictates of secular society, against a backdrop of excessive individualism. Taken together these amount to rejection of the trustworthiness of many groups of people, both inside and outside the church, and a general fear of the unknown. For many, antipathy to authority and being instructed to behave in a certain way has led to resolute rejection of vaccine mandates, regardless of the health-based justification for them. When Christians respond in this manner, it is legitimate to ask what Christian values are prompting this response. Indeed, are they expressions of Christian values aimed at helping the vulnerable and underprivileged?

The rejection of mainstream thinking on vaccines is a multifaceted social problem especially when manifested by highly-trained health professionals being sucked into gross misinformation, and even more by those who are prepared to sacrifice their careers and families over a vaccine. This is doubly perplexing when found in Christian communities, since in these instances the impression that is being given is that they are allowing their response to a vaccine to become a dominant factor in their faith.

The trouble with so much of this debate was that the dangers of the COVID virus were underplayed or even overlooked while dependence upon misinformation found on the internet overrode even the merest respect for local experts including experts in their own churches. This raised the possibility that there were unseen spiritual forces at work, aided and abetted by false teaching.

Year 3: Towards an Uncertain Future

A well-worn expression since the beginning of the pandemic is that we can look forward to the "new normal." This is based on the presumption that the availability of an effective vaccine enables everyone to return to normal existence. Even if it is the so-called "new normal," in essence it is back to the old normal of absolute control over the forces of nature. But this outlook has hit a number of snags. The first is that the task of vaccinating vast impoverished populations in Africa and Asia has proved far more momentous than generally realized, requiring a willingness on the part of the high- and upper-middle-income countries to support the poorest and most vulnerable people by ensuring that adequate supplies of vaccines are made available at minimal cost. To date, this has failed in spite of the best intentions of the vaccine sharing policy COVAX, with the goal of global equitable access to COVID-19 vaccines. It appears that enough doses are being produced globally but these are not being distributed equitably. In other words, the tools to bring the pandemic under control are available, but the will is not there on the part of the countries and companies that control the global supply to prioritize supply to COVAX and provide worldwide access to vaccines. Additionally, the organizational and physical resources are not available in many countries where the health services are rudimentary. The result is that the virus will continue to mutate, cross borders, and wreak havoc for everyone across the world.

This represents a major failure of political will and ethical priorities, due in no small part to small-mindedness, selfishness, and self-centeredness. The task for Christians is obvious, to do all in their power to point to the fundamentals of the faith—living for others, serving others, and supporting them in every way possible. The present situation is both appallingly self-centered and scientifically disastrous. All suffer for as long as there are numerous unvaccinated people in many countries. This is a clear demonstration of our failure to realize the oneness of the human race.

A Christian input is crucial when dealing with public health emergencies, since the focus moves from the individual to the community, from my welfare to the welfare of those around me. When asked what is the greatest commandment Jesus reminded his listeners that it is to love God with every element of their being and to love their neighbor as themselves (Matt 22:37–39; Mark 12:30–31). On another occasion, in response to the question of who is my neighbor, Jesus responded with the parable of the good Samaritan (Luke 10:25–37). The surprising and even shocking aspect of this story is that those who would have been expected to assist walked on, leaving an alien, a Samaritan, to help and look after him. Together, these two incidents highlight the importance of looking after others, our neighbors, whoever they may be, any who may be affected by our actions and our attitudes, in our communities and farther afield.

Year 3 and beyond will not be, and is not, the sort of normal we have become accustomed to over many years. In order to tackle it adequately, we have to take far more seriously the fundamental truth that the world of which we are a part is broken, and the important question for Christians is to ask what humans can do to rectify that which has gone wrong and correct these problems to the best of our abilities. We are to help where we can help and correct where we can correct. We should thank God for the awe-inspiring power of our bodily immune system and for the doctors and researchers who have developed vaccines to strengthen that system.

If nothing else, a pandemic should have brought home to the church that science is one of God's momentous gifts in providing a means of healing when confronted by a virus gone awry. There is nothing new in this, since Christians have historically played a strategic and valiant part in setting up hospitals and providing healthcare resources in one country after another for century after century. The tragedy is that a minority of Christians has been led astray by mischievous claims that originate elsewhere and lack any basis in careful scientific research and reputable evidence. Ignoring the place of the mind in God's economy is a dereliction of the Christian's responsibility to please him and serve him faithfully (Rom 12:1–2; see chapter 9).

A scientific approach is crucial when confronted with a creation that is broken and is groaning in its brokenness. In Christian terms, public health and allied measures contribute to a partial restoration of creation, including the partial redemption of the bodies of human beings. A central calling of Christians is to support these efforts, within which there is a central role for experts in public health, epidemiology, and virology. These have their part to play within that part of the mission field dedicated to bringing and restoring health.

Now that the worst of the pandemic may be behind us (but that depends on where one is located in the world), it is tempting to ask whether these last two chapters have any ongoing relevance. Have they simply become historic relics, carrying little more than curious interest? Perhaps these chapters could have been omitted from the book, as we move on with the other science-faith questions that tickle our fancy and intrigue us intellectually. My response is that it would be foolish to think and act in this manner. The pandemic has provided Christians with a unique opportunity to reflect on the practical relationship between their faith and the science that impinges upon it. It has also brought to light controversies that should disturb Christians as they reflect on how seriously they do or do not take their task to seek to live as servants, thinking and behaving in ways that will benefit their communities. The pattern laid out by Jesus in his life and supremely in his death should serve as a goad to Christians to utilize the scientific expertise at their fingertips to promote the good of others rather than their own interests.

5

Cystic Fibrosis

Looking to Science for Hope

Exploring a Little-Known Disease

THERE IS A DISTINCT personal element in this chapter since I am dealing with a disease that is in my own family. I am aware that writing in this manner has dangers: I am too close and hence too emotionally involved; I am biased and my assessment of what can and should be done for those with this condition—cystic fibrosis (CF)—will be unbalanced. All this is true, and yet, as my account will make clear, it is individuals and families in a similar situation who have been responsible for making possible huge strides in uncovering the mechanisms that result in CF and have to be adjusted if treatments are to found that will alleviate this condition. It also demonstrates that I am a person with human concerns and commitments. It brings my human side to the surface rather than my academic side. I am a person of faith who has to cope with illness and genetic defects in his own family and not just in other families. I cannot be a mere theoretician, even if I wanted to be. My aim is to bring to the surface some of the Christian-faith connotations of a potentially debilitating lifelong condition that I cannot keep at arm's length.[1]

This one condition can be taken as a model for many other congenital, relatively rare conditions, treatment of which is dependent upon scientific and medical insights that are hard won and come at a cost. Examples abound,

1. Much of this chapter is based on an article of mine: Jones, "Cystic Fibrosis, Trikafta and Christian Hope."

Cystic Fibrosis

from achondroplasia and a number of lysosomal storage diseases to Marfan syndrome and neurofibromatosis. In each of these conditions, healing is highly dependent upon understanding the underlying mechanisms causing the disease and the effectiveness of the technological approaches available to alleviate the worst effects of the condition. In each case, we are confronted by the importance of scientific approaches aimed at making sense of the disease, dependence upon the science in producing workable therapies, and recognition of the grace of God in all these developments.

A Personal Encounter with Cystic Fibrosis

The unexpected arrival of a child or grandchild with CF is an event with untold ramifications. Chronic ill health is inevitable, as is a relatively short lifespan. The quality of life is detrimentally affected, and huge efforts are required to make possible relatively normal life; much of this is science-based. Additionally, the costs are huge, mainly in the development of potent drugs, quite apart from the myriad hospital appointments and daily therapies. All these in their various ways have emerged from extensive scientific research and have the potential of bringing about dramatic changes for the better in many CF patients.

A significant finding has been that treatment needs to be commenced as early as possible, preferably from birth. In some instances, the latter follows seamlessly, since bowel obstruction within the first day or so of birth is a frequent indicator of CF. Traumatic as this is at the time, since it is the result of a build-up of meconium and increased viscosity of intestinal mucus, it precipitates early treatment. Genetic analysis is required to confirm the diagnosis. Early treatment means that it can limit the severity of lung damage.

Cystic fibrosis is the most common autosomal recessive cause of early mortality in Caucasians and is caused by a recessive gene that manifests itself when both parents are carriers. Around one in twenty-five people in the population are carriers, although most are unaware of their carrier status. When both parents are carriers, the chance of having a child with CF is 25 percent. This is due to a defective protein that results from mutations in the gene encoding the cystic fibrosis transmembrane regulator (CFTR). These mutations reduce the release of chloride ions in epithelial tissues, and hyperactivate the epithelial sodium channels that aid in the absorption of sodium ions.[2]

---

2. Drew, "Research Round-up: Cystic Fibrosis," S18–19. Also Almughem et al.,

The result is that the mucus becomes dehydrated and thickened, making it suitable for bacterial growth. While most attention focuses on the lungs, other organs are also affected, including the pancreas, liver, gallbladder, and intestines; the reproductive system; and the sweat glands. In the lungs the thick sticky mucus leads to shortness of breath, a chronic cough, and repeated chest infections; in the pancreas it reduces or stops enzymes from being released into the gastrointestinal tract to digest food, causing problems with poor weight gain and malnutrition due to malabsorption. People with CF lose large amounts of salt, reflected in sweat that is very salty.[3]

In light of this wide variety of affected bodily systems, CF sufferers have to take numerous daily medications, including intensive antibiotic therapy and aerosols, along with constant physiotherapy. They eat extra food, gorging on fatty foods, and benefit by exercising vigorously. In the absence of effective therapy, the disease advances inexorably, necessitating an increasing frequency of hospitalizations. Consequently, with increasing age, there is a downward trajectory unless this can be stopped by vigorous effective treatment. The goal of this treatment is to minimize lung damage for as long as possible and hold off the day when a double lung transplant becomes the only feasible option (see *The Use of Science in the Service of Those with CF*, 85–88, for a far brighter outlook).

Around 70,000 individuals worldwide have CF. The lack of currently available technology in the twentieth century meant that children with CF rarely survived for more than a few years. For instance, at the time when the genetic disorder was first discovered in the 1930s, 80 percent of children born with CF died before the age of one. By 1970, life expectancy had risen to around twelve years of age. The first drug developed specifically for CF was approved in 1993. Today, the median life expectancy of people with CF is closer to forty, although this varies considerably from one country to another, depending upon the treatments available and affordable. Very starkly, if our grandchild had been born forty years before he was, when highly sophisticated facilities were not available, and if the substantial costs could not have been met, he would have died during early childhood. As it is, his future lifespan and the quality of his life are dependent upon continuation of the constantly improving treatments available to him and the

---

"Cystic Fibrosis," 616.

3. Yankaskas et al., "Cystic Fibrosis Adult Care." Also Davis, "Cystic Fibrosis since 1938."

extent to which this treatment can be further improved by the availability of ongoing genetically-based drugs.

The individual with CF has a chronic illness and has never experienced a period of wellness, stability, or perceived normality. Interestingly, though, children and young people with CF tend to say, "I've never not had it so I don't really know what it's like not to." They are not blind, they do not have any intellectual disability, they are not in a wheelchair, they can communicate normally, and they probably do not look much different from anyone else. And yet they exist on an intensive medical regime, their lifespan is much less than that of their counterparts, and they will experience hospitalizations far more than most other people. They are also advised not to interact with other CF children in order to minimize the chances of passing on serious infections to one another.

While the severity of CF varies considerably, depending upon which genetic deletion individuals have, the activities of many of them are restricted. For many there will be annual hospitalizations of one to two weeks, the ongoing daily treatment regime is, as referred to above, invasive, the dietary regime is intrusive, and the prospect of a lung transplant is ever-present for some of them. Their schooling is interfered with, and there is no escape from the unending pressure placed on family and siblings. Those with CF are disabled; they are unable to perform some activities considered to be within the normal functional range.[4]

A Disease without a Cure

There is no cure, no matter how revolutionary some of the scientific advances of recent years have been. Well-meaning people continue to ask, "When will he be better?" or within a Christian setting, "God will cure him. Just pray for a miracle." The intentions may be exemplary, but they are unhelpfully misguided. They fail to grasp the reality that there will be no overnight cure or "get-out-of-jail card." The clinical trajectory will be downhill unless it can be halted by stunning new technological insights or, at the very least, substantially retarded. The immense progress in understanding the genetic mechanisms underlying CF, and in light of this finding ways of countering these mechanisms and reversing their clinical manifestations, is a reason for hope grounded in evidence-based reality. The truth is, though, that the hope is greatest for the very young, those born within the last few years.

4. Jones, "The World of Cystic Fibrosis," 21–31.

The drain on the parents and family is considerable and unending. Looking after a child with CF has repercussions for other children in the family since far more attention has to be directed towards the one who is ill with their immediate medical needs. On occasion what can and cannot be done on family holidays is controlled by the one at the expense of the others. The CF child lives with constant monitoring and treatment and hospital appointments. The support of parents, family, and friends is crucial, more so if the CF is debilitating. The difficulty is that these impediments increase as the child becomes a teenager and as the teenager moves into young adulthood. The pressure on the family is immense, particularly if two children in the family have CF. This provides the context for the decision whether to have another, or a further, child (see *Decision-Making in the Midst of the Family*, 82–85).

Against this background, it is imperative to ask how Christians respond to a condition like this, and, more to the point, how does one respond to a child with this condition? The immediate response is to say that this is a child like any other, to be loved and cared for, to be encouraged and supported just as one would support any other child and growing adult. This is fine, but it does no more than scratch the surface. We need to start from the premise that this is God's world and children are a gift from God, regardless of any biological "deficiencies" or "imperfections." All are to be loved and cared for. This the basis for stating that everything possible is to be done to assist them, even though the sad realization is that what is feasible varies hugely from one country to another and even from one area to another within the same country. Children with the same condition and theoretically with the same life chances will have the opportunity to prosper in one situation but not in another. Much of this stems from the levels of government funding for very expensive drug regimes. No decision-making is straightforward, and many competing forces come into play, politically, socially, and culturally, leading to inequality and unfairness from which none of us can escape.

The Christian has the opportunity to advocate for as much equality as can be achieved. This will range from advocating for high-quality public health systems open to all, especially those with limited means, to providing for a wide spectrum of disease conditions, including unglamorous ones like behavioral and mental health conditions such as fetal alcohol spectrum disorder (FASD). I would like to see churches supporting those with expertise in these areas, encouraging them as they strive to direct attention at the need for improvements in health and welfare services. This can be a very unrewarding task, as one agency comes up against another and as the needs of those all too readily ignored by society seem to stall as they come up against almost impenetrable barriers. Many of these conditions are long-term ones, meaning that support often has to be sustained for decades.

Christians are to be grateful for what is made available, scientifically, socially, and communally, because all these are blessings from God. The work of research scientists, doctors, and other healthcare workers is to be welcomed as an outcome of God's providence and grace. It may not be totally inappropriate to look back at the way in which God provided for the Israelites through the manna and quail in the desert. Different as were the circumstances then, God provided for them as long as they followed his directions about when to eat it and as they learned to trust God for his provisions (Exod 16:1–36). Human agency should always be seen alongside God's providential action, since we are to learn that he has provided the means by which human beings are to respond to vicissitudes, of which CF on the one hand and a pandemic on the other are just two illustrations. Putting to good use the scientific means at our disposal is a positive response to God's overtures; it is the very antithesis of rebellion or unjustified use of our autonomy. In similar vein, we are to show gratitude when a society is stable, with political and health systems that strive to be equitable and make therapies accessible to those who potentially are able to benefit most from them, regardless of the ability to pay.

Church communities need to learn to support parents looking after children with chronic illnesses, since the ongoing demands on their time and resources can be very steep and draining. Support, if it is to be really helpful, has to be long-term but is nothing less than a crucial outworking of gospel imperatives. The example provided by the early churches' support for widows in need constitutes a useful blueprint (1 Tim 5:3–16). Some of these were in real need, a category that today would include CF, whereas others were not. This distinction is helpful in approaching some diseases but is unlikely to apply to the latest breakthrough drug combination for CF, where all who could benefit using medical (genetic) criteria fit the category of being in real need (see *The Use of Science in the Service of Those with CF*, 85–88).

At the Margins

Decision-Making in the Midst of the Family

The chance of having a second child with CF is one in four, just as it was for the first child (or a previous child with CF). On this occasion, though, the parents are faced with having to make a decision: should they have another child when the chances of having one with CF are one in four? Can they adequately look after two children with CF should the latest addition also have CF? Can they love both sufficiently, and would they regard another child with CF as a "gift of God"? They have no qualms about how much they love their child with CF, but are they capable of having another child who will make yet more demands on them and on their lives together? As Christians they also realize there are very practical theological questions, notably, their dependence upon God and his care for them. They can see four possible ways forward.[5]

1. They could decide against having another child; the one-in-four prospect of another child with CF is more than they think they would be able to bear. They also do not want to bring into the world another individual with a distressing condition like CF.

2. They could proceed with a pregnancy as though nothing had happened and CF was not in their family. They simply take a chance in the hope that all will be well. As Christians they might argue that the welfare of their next child is in God's hands regardless of the outcome.

3. They could take a chance, knowing that an abortion is a possibility if the fetus, when genetically tested, turns out to be affected. However, they are concerned that this course of action would send the message that their existing child should never have been born.

4. They could resort to using IVF and PGD (pre-implantation genetic diagnosis). If this showed that an embryo at the four- or eight-cell stage was not carrying the CF gene, it would be transferred to the woman in the normal way (see chapter 6). On the other hand, if the embryo was carrying the CF gene, that embryo would be discarded and the same procedure would be carried out on another embryo and so on until an embryo lacking this gene was found.

For a couple in this situation there is no escape from the reality of CF and its profound effects on any children they bring into existence. They

---

5. Jones, "The World of Cystic Fibrosis," 26–28.

Cystic Fibrosis

have to make a decision, even if it is not to make a decision! They will have decided to have no further children, to have a child with or without CF, or they will have produced embryos or fetuses that will have been discarded either as embryos or aborted as fetuses. These are invidious choices, but there is no escape for a couple in this situation who are thinking about having further children. Christians will be in the same quandary as others, and the pertinent question is to ask whether they have additional resources based upon Scripture. What factors might this couple take into account?

The first option raises issues associated with self-inflicted childlessness—albeit for well-intentioned reasons. Are they taking too much control into their own hands? They might argue that they have done this repeatedly, since they use contraceptives. Non-technological as this response is, it is not leaving everything in the hands of God.

Turning to the second possibility, going ahead and hoping that their next child will not have CF, in spite of the relatively high odds of having such a child, could be interpreted in one of two ways. The parents accept that God can use both illness and ongoing limitations for good. This may be viewed as the pathway of faith. Over against this, by rejecting some of the avenues opened up by scientific advance, they are prepared to allow into the world an individual with a well-recognized disease. Striking a balance between these two is a matter of discernment and will come down to personal perspectives and priorities.

The third path of resorting to an abortion in the face of a positive diagnosis of CF is highly problematic for most Christians because of its willingness to abort a fetus with CF. It gives the impression of being life-denying and a substantial threat to the perceived value of the existing child with CF. It may also send a message to other disabled people that their lives are not worth living.

The final option, with its dependence upon IVF and PGD, is the path of technological utilization. Quite apart from the financial costs involved, it is invasive and involves the selection of embryos. It is explicit in its reliance upon choosing one embryo over another, and inevitably on destroying some embryos that have the potential to develop into living individuals (albeit with CF). It highlights two competing values—embryos versus other participants, including the future child. This direction differs from the previous one, that of abortion, since it is less obviously life-denying and is positive in that it utilizes to the full technological knowledge and skills. Inevitably, though, it is an ambiguous choice.

Whichever direction is taken, Christian couples need to ask themselves how best God can be glorified in their situation and through their actions. What resources do they possess to assist them in this very demanding position? Consider the following. They are to protect the defenseless and the disenfranchised, they are to stress the importance of human flourishing, and all these are within the context of their ultimate dependence upon God. Jesus came to proclaim good news to the oppressed, and human life is not devoid of meaning simply because it is physically flawed. They also need to take on board the transformative power of the physical and spiritual healing that Jesus brought and that can be experienced today in the midst of Christian community. Alongside these considerations they are to be grateful for the manner in which medical achievements bring hope and new prospects in the midst of illness.[6]

There is no inevitability about any one conclusion, but these points constitute the framework for decision-making. What is in the best interests of the family as a whole, the existing child with CF, any future children who may exist with or without CF, and possibly any embryos? The weight placed on each of these will depend on many factors, and the balance achieved between these frequently conflicting interests should reflect the diverse relationships that characterize the family, the human community, and the church community.

All options are enshrined in uncertainty. The IVF/PGD route entails disposal of the affected embryos. This is not inevitable and they could decide it is a step too far. They could avoid going down this technological route by not having any further children or simply not thinking about the consequences of having another child. But they should not delude themselves by thinking that remaining ignorant is a virtue. That is not a viable option for Christians who have been given freedom in Christ (Gal 5:13–25), freedom to follow his dictates and use the abilities and resources provided by human creativity. They are to be stewards of God's good creation. Ignorance is not a virtue when confronted by malaria, tuberculosis, or dysentery, let alone by measles or smallpox, about which something can be done in all these cases. Failure to act in these circumstances is an evil that blights everyone. Similarly, ignorance in the face of CF is not a virtue, neither for the parents faced by these options nor for the CF community and the opportunities opened up by scientific research.

---

6. See the writings of Allen Verhey, including *Reading the Bible in the Strange World of Medicine* and "What Makes Christian Bioethics Christian?"

An addendum to this discussion came into public gaze at the time of writing. A leading Australian politician, known for his Christian position, made the comment that he and his wife were "blessed" that they did not have disabled children. While this statement was made in the heat of a leaders' debate, and while it may have been partly taken out of context, the words with their Christian allusion of being blessed created intense disquiet. Is it true that those with disabled children are not blessed by God, and is it right to think we are blessed by having healthy children? At the very least it seemed to reflect an "ableist" mindset and that disabled children are burdens, even though this was probably not the politician's intended message.

As we have seen in the case of CF, there can be no question that disabled children may present considerable burdens no matter how much they are loved and cared for. There may be immense challenges, especially if families having to cope with them have limited resources and few support mechanisms. From this we conclude that the Christian response is to provide as much support as feasible and to advocate for communal and government support. If we believe in the equality of all God's children, it is imperative that we strive to operationalize this by providing what is needed. In functioning in this manner, the church can be a blessing as it shows love and offers practical assistance.

The origin of this concern was a debate about the future of the country's National Disability Insurance Scheme and the provisions made available within society, from wheelchair ramps, accessible transport, and automatic doors to sophisticated medications as in CF. These are scientific devises that serve to allow those with disabilities to lead as "normal" lives as possible, allowing them to realize their full potential and to varying degrees leveling the playfield with their non-disabled compatriots.

The Use of Science in the Service of Those with Cystic Fibrosis

Approaches to CF take us into a world of vigorous multi-disciplinary research, as attempts are made to devise increasingly effective therapies. These are aimed at i) circumventing CF-related ion transport defects pharmacologically; ii) finding ways of correcting the basic defect in cells in what is known as a chloride channel (CFTR, the CF transmembrane conductance regulator); and iii) using gene therapy to insert a normal copy of the CF gene into affected cells.

At the Margins

The costs of research over the past forty or so years have been extraordinarily high (in the billions of dollars), but it has been the range and nature of this research that has been responsible for what have been truly transformative results. In other words, the quality of life of most patients with CF is completely dependent upon sophisticated science and technology. This is not an option but a necessity. Science and technology are enabling individuals with CF to realize far more of their potential as human beings than would otherwise be possible. In a small way, CF is reminiscent of the plight of the whole creation, that has been subjected to frustration, is groaning as in the pains of childbirth, and is longing to be liberated from its bondage to decay (Rom 8:20–25). This longing is eloquently displayed in the lives and trials of young people with CF.

The initial description of CF in 1938 was followed by a quiescent period until in 1953 it was realized that people with CF have excessively salty sweat.[7] This innocuous-sounding observation provided clues about what was probably happening in the cells. This led to thirty years of scientific progress, driven to a large degree by those with personal experience of having children with CF, and supported by philanthropists and diverse groups of scientists with a fascinating mix of complementary disciplinary skills. Consequently, it was advocates for CF children and their families who made conspicuous strides with both the scientific work and the philanthropy on which it was heavily dependent. But it was not all hype, because just beneath the surface there were tragedies, as children with CF were dying at early ages—in their teens and earlier. And in some instances, it was not just one child in a family who had CF, but two and very occasionally three. On some occasions all died early deaths. Life expectancy during the 1950s through the 1970s was low, with children usually dying by their teens. What stands out from these years are the huge costs required to undertake the scientific work, most of which was privately sourced, the ability of those behind the various CF foundations to repeatedly raise countless millions of dollars, and the creativity and commitment of scientists from a wide range of biomedical disciplines.

Major breakthroughs began first with the discovery of the CF gene in 1989. One of the main geneticists behind this discovery was Francis Collins (see chapter 3). It then became possible to understand and subsequently

---

7. Much of this account is based on data provided by Trivedi, *Breath from Salt: A Deadly Genetic Disease, a New Era in Science, and the Patients and Families Who Changed Medicine Forever*.

find means of unraveling the cellular defects in CF. Each of these discoveries involved vast swathes of work that were far from straightforward as it encountered one problem and disappointment after another. However, a therapeutics development program was initiated, with efforts directed towards developing drugs that would correct the non-functioning CFTR protein. The ultimate goal was to find a cure for CF, but at present that remains elusive.

As this work progressed what became glaringly obvious was that the errors underlying the symptoms of CF are complex. For instance, there are approximately two thousand known mutations of the CFTR gene, the most common of which is the F508del mutation. The challenges posed by this complexity have become evident over recent years as concerted attempts have been made to understand the disease and its mechanisms and sketch ways of subsequently correcting the disorders. Progress has been gradual but also meaningful, with consistent increases in life expectancy each year. Additionally, as drugs of increasing efficacy became available, morbidity declined.

There are different groups of CF patients based on the different mutations they possess. This means that drugs have to be designed very precisely so that they can correct different sets of mutations. As this was done, clinical trials were conducted at each stage to test their efficacy. Gradually, an increasing array of drugs was formulated, each being directed at a particular genetic mutation and cellular error. By 2008, it became apparent that it is possible to treat the root cause of CF, leading in 2012 to FDA approval of Kalydeco for a number of specific, but largely rare, CF mutations (G551D) that affect 4–8 percent of CF sufferers.

Further steps were taken in 2015 with FDA approval of Orkambi for people with two copies of the common F508del mutation, then in 2019 Symdeko (tezacaftor and ivacaftor tablets) and finally Trikafta (elexacaftor, tezacaftor, and ivacaftor tablets), as the first triple-combination therapy for those with the most common and most severe type of CF. Each new drug represented a distinct advance in the efficacy of treatment, culminating in Trikafta, with its potential for revolutionizing the health status of a large number of individuals with CF. Over the years, numerous combinations of molecules were tested through all three phases of clinical trials, with each molecule working on a different part of the CFTR protein. The aim in all cases was to restore the balance of salt and water in the lung, pancreas, gut, and sweat glands.[8]

8. Jones, "Cystic Fibrosis, Trikafta and Christian Hope," 4.

This combination of drugs, as Trikafta, marks the beginning of a new era of genetic medicine.[9] It is approved for patients twelve years and older who have at least one F508del mutation in the CFTR gene and accounts for 90 percent of the CF population. Its three component drugs each target different regions in the defective CFTR protein. The goal is to enable the protein affected by the CFTR gene mutation to function more effectively. When successful, the broken channel in the CFTR protein is fixed with a synthetic molecule that in turn changes a patient's entire physiology from the saltiness of their skin to the volume of air in their lungs.

This progression was based on gradually increasing knowledge of the pathology underlying CF and how it might be rectified. Each new drug was designed to perform a particular function and overcome a specific error in the mechanisms controlling the movement of chloride ions into and out of cells. The driving force has been to understand the basic cellular errors giving rise to CF. This is exceedingly methodical science at all levels from the cellular to the clinical, made possible by remarkable human ingenuity and driven by the needs of patients and their families.

The reason for outlining these details is to provide insight into the precision of the research work, as well as the minuscule deficiencies in the CFTR protein, that cause the massive clinical problems for those with CF. This is scientific investigation at its best, particularly as its goal is to correct pathologies in a vulnerable population. This in my estimation is the essence of a faithful response to creative abilities bestowed upon human beings by God. The trajectory of these developments is not found in every area of biomedicine, but its brilliance in this instance is nothing less than a thing of beauty and wonder.

Reflections on the Science-Faith Duopoly

I have indicated my bias towards those with CF because of my family connection. The developments outlined above can be viewed simply as a case study in some of the remarkable achievements of medical science in providing hope for a relatively small number of patients at enormous expense.

---

9. The details are beyond the reach of this chapter, although it is worth noting them since they demonstrate the intricacy of the research. Different molecules correct different anomalies in the CFTR protein, that is, VX-661 is the "corrector" in Symdeko; VX-770 is the "doorman" in Kalydeco; VX-659 (VX-445) is a second "corrector." Together, this combination, in the form of Trikaftor, was found to resurrect the broken CFTR protein.

One interpretation is that this is science and medical treatment for the elite. But that would be unfair; CF affects individuals across the whole spectrum of society, and their lives are equally affected by the genetic deletion they have. All should be offered healing if available. Not only this, but the approaches developed in this research will eventually percolate through to other conditions, including very common ones.

No one would expect to find exact parallels in Scripture, although the healing of the blind man is useful (John 9:1–41). This man's condition had been present from birth, just as CF is present from birth. Jesus was clear: neither this man nor his parents had sinned, but it provided Jesus with an opportunity to heal him. And this is exactly what he did, using materials at his disposal. For Jesus this was an opportunity for the works of God to be displayed in and through this man, whose life was transformed by Jesus. His simple exclamation is spine tingling: "I was blind but now I see" (John 9:24). There are a number of instructive lessons here: there is a place for the healing of congenital conditions, there is a role for physical (scientific/medical) intervention, and God can be glorified through physical healing. Christians should find hope in healing, and they should rejoice when illness is successfully combatted.

There is no virtue in blindness if it can be healed; if not, ways have to be found of accepting it and responding to it in as positive a manner as possible. Similarly, there is no virtue in CF if it can be healed, or, as is the case today, in subduing its worst manifestations. The many attempts at gradually understanding the basic cellular failures in CF do not signify a lack of faith on the part of Christians; they illustrate the use of God-given abilities to rectify pathologies that mar so much that is beautiful in God's world.

Christians start from the basis that this is God's world, a basis that allows no room for any sacred-secular divide or a science-faith dichotomy. The world we encounter is God's handiwork, an integral part of which are the lives and actions of human beings, with responsibility for ourselves and our environment. This includes the privileged task of being co-creators with God in improving conditions and rectifying what has gone wrong (Ps 8:5–8; Heb 2:6–8). Our overwhelming response should be gratitude for the many ways in which we and others can assist those in need of healing, using the creative abilities bestowed upon us to improve the health and prospects of patients, CF in this instance. Central to these abilities is the power of science and its clinical applications. This follows on from the well-known trajectory of Christian healthcare throughout the ages. It is putting science to good use in showing love for one's neighbor and in seeking to rectify all that is threatening and destructive (Mark 12:30–31; Jas 1:27).

God's purposes in helping broken people depend in part on scientific input. This is vital to his providential purposes. Acknowledging that science is not always put to good uses in no way contradicts this important theme. Scientists are as broken as the rest of humankind, but, like all others, the good frequently shines through. In the case of CF and the vast amount of research put into understanding the mechanisms of action of an aberrant gene, the motives have been exemplary, driven as they have been by concern for the sick and striving to uncover means of remedying the sickness.

Each scientific project is to be assessed on its merits, using the biblical adage that "you will know them by their fruits" (Matt 7:16–20). A simple touchstone is that God's care and human care are to be in harmony, each directed towards the same ends. Being mindful of God's care serves to remind us that what is important is the way in which we care for others, the complete antithesis of seeking to control others and have power over them. The scientific work behind CF had as its goal the prospect of adding value to the life experiences of these children and young adults, thereby enhancing all they are as those who image God and providing them with a better way.

When science is utilized in this manner, the scientists behind it are to be applauded, recognizing that they are fulfilling God's purposes in healing, regardless of whether or not they recognize this. Such has been the case with the multitude of attempts to understand and come to terms with CF. But even here there is a warning: science must never be elevated to the status of an idol. In this instance, science has been driven by a longing for healing, a welcome motive. But the healing will be partial and inevitably temporary. Nevertheless, while it is right to be reminded of these limitations, this is not an excuse to downplay the contribution of science within God's purposes: on one condition, that it is being directed towards enhancement of God's creation.

What about the Cost of the Drugs?

The enormous developmental costs cannot be ignored, and there is little point in devising therapies, especially fundamentally transformational ones, if they are too expensive to be used by the patients for whom they were designed. This is an ethical conundrum with theological ramifications.

As pointed out previously, the costs of Trikafta are extraordinarily high, raising the question of whether those suffering from CF and their parents can legitimately expect such costs to be covered by the public purse. For Christians, the concerns touch on fairness; is this treatment to be confined to the privileged? Of course, this question is far from unique, since it applies to other conditions with very expensive treatments. They appear repeatedly when confronted by potentially effective and highly innovative treatments for a range of conditions, from heart transplants to gene-targeting therapies. There has been prolonged debate over this, and the problems are likely to increase as more scientific breakthroughs come onto the market. The trouble is that the costs of drug development, clinical trials, and production often run into mouth-watering figures, namely, billions of dollars. To make matters even more complex, the costs are often borne not just by the pharmaceutical companies themselves but by universities and hence public money, and also by private money. When patents expire, costs can be reduced when generic and biosimilar drugs become available, but these prospects lie in the future.

A tragedy is afoot when drug treatments are available but cannot be accessed by those who potentially could benefit from them on the grounds of cost. This, unfortunately, is not a new problem but is highlighted by exceptionally expensive drugs designed specifically to treat very serious conditions. A crucial consideration is how much health benefit they can be expected to provide. Is this a few weeks or months of better quality of life for adults, or is it many years of good health for young people who otherwise would die at a young age? The moral imperative for the latter is far more pressing than for the former, no matter how much one would always like to be able to improve an individual's wellbeing. This is a challenge in high-income countries, where it is regularly the subject of debate. But this ignores the far bigger challenge for low-income countries, where there is insufficient support for routine, let alone ground-breaking, treatment. While that situation, valid as it is, lies outside the scope of this chapter, it should never be sidelined by Christians.

Returning to the CF/Trikafta situation, the task for Christians is whether Trikafta, or any other exceedingly expensive treatment, will enable those receiving it to more clearly mirror their design as one of God's creations? Will the treatment bring glory to God through healing? In these terms, Trikafta emerges positively, although pressure needs to be brought on the drug company to ensure that it is not being exploitative in seeking to maximize its profits by charging whatever prices it thinks the market will bear. Hyper-expensive treatment, such as that exemplified by Trikafta, promises a reasonable standard of health for many, if not all, CF patients for a large number of life-years, and with it the prospect of developing into flourishing adults.

But even with such a transformative procedure as that offered by Trikafta, there is ambiguity. Even such a transformative drug lacks magical powers; there are side effects, and some individuals will not benefit because of them. It also fails to address some gene combinations. Realism is crucial, since even the most sophisticated biomedical science will let us down, and some young people with CF will continue to die at a tragically young age. We constantly have to ask where God is to be found even when the treatment fails or may be unavailable. Technology alone will never answer every query about decline and death, and it should never be expected to do so. This is transcending the boundaries of science. Trikafta, with all its stupendous results, will not lead to an illness-free existence, but neither is this to denigrate its potential benefits and substantial blessings.

Christian thinking faces up to the inevitability of suffering and mortality not in a fatalistic way but by seeking to be faithful to Christ in the midst of suffering. When confronted by suffering and an uncertain future, the Christian is to examine the technology available and the manner in which it might be used to assist in this situation. Use it if appropriate, but never fail to ask whether this is the way of Christ in these circumstances and with this condition.[10]

Trikafta is genetic medicine at its best. This has nothing to do with ushering in the new Jerusalem or, for those opposed to any genetic interventions, precipitating Armageddon. Such scenarios have far more to do with science fiction than with clinical and research reality. They are deeply misleading. The example of Trikafta and CF throws the spotlight onto the reality of human suffering and of stunning medical improvements. A basis in science and medicine is frequently a good place to start for theological analysis by centering on an evidence-based approach.

Trikafta is a basis for Christian hope not in the sense that it solves all the problems of those with CF but as an indication of how God works through his creation and the gifts he has bestowed upon human beings. It is one means by which he restores a broken world. It is a sign of hope when approached through the looking glass of the redemption made possible by

---

10. See further discussions of mine in: "The Changing Face of the Science-Faith Dialogue in a Biomedical Arena," 165–75; and *The Peril and Promise of Medical Technology*, 231, 233.

Christ and the eternal hope that stems from what he did on the cross and in being raised from the dead.[11]

Learning from Cystic Fibrosis

Some of the material in this chapter was first given at a conference on disability. Since my coverage of CF was quite different from the conditions covered by others in the conference—cognitive impairment, schizophrenia, cerebral palsy—I was forced to consider whether CF is a disability since many definitions of disability do not include CF. I argued that it is a disability for a number reasons.[12]

The first is that any definition of disability should be broad enough to encompass conditions that at times are far from obvious to outsiders. The need for constant support is sufficient to warrant use of the term and should not be reserved simply for those occasions when there is hospitalization or particularly intensive therapy. At such times the individual with CF gives the appearance of being disabled even if at other times that is not the case.

The second is that a disabling condition such as CF can, in principle, be alleviated by the application of cutting-edge innovative therapies. As I have already argued, these are to be welcomed by people of faith, since their goal is improving the lot of individuals made in the image of God. The individual's disability will not have been removed, but rectifying it partially is a blessing to be cherished and celebrated as a gift from God.

In the third place, it is unhelpful to view disabilities in a homogeneous manner. There is no one single stance on dealing with disabilities and those who are disabled. There are substantial differences between CF on the one hand and Down Syndrome on the other, and social attitudes towards the two differ substantially. These have ethical and theological implications, such as the validity of employing non-invasive prenatal testing (NIPT). The concern is that they open the door to knowledge that may lead to halting the ongoing development of certain embryos and the individuals they would have become. This prospect has quite different repercussions in the one situation compared with the other, dependent upon the ethical and cultural perspectives of those making the decisions rather than upon the science.

My aim in this chapter has been to focus on one condition and explore the degree to which scientific and technological approaches can be

11. Jones, "Cystic Fibrosis, Trikafta and Christian Hope," 6–7.
12. Jones, "The World of Cystic Fibrosis," 30–31.

life-enhancing. The simple message is that there is no escape from the contribution of scientific tools in this condition, as in many others. To reject what science has to offer is to reject one of God's gifts to human beings living in a broken world. It is a means made available by God as part of his providential dealings with his creation.

6

The Embryo, the Reproductive Technologies, and Christian Faithfulness

Facing Up to a "No-Go" Area

MY STANCE ON A range of bioethical questions has been regarded as problematic within more conservative Christian circles, with the opposition circling around my position on the status of the human embryo (chapter 1). While I have never wished to concentrate on this topic, and while I have never regarded it as of preeminent concern, this is where I have deviated from what is seen in some quarters as a crucial landmark of faithfulness to the biblical revelation.

Gradually over the years, from the 1970s and 1980s onwards, there has been a hardening of attitudes towards the status of the embryo within conservative Christian circles. What was of theoretical interest, and subsidiary to the abortion debate, has come to occupy a central place in biomedicine. Very simply, the embryo has emerged from the obscurity of women's bodies into the light of the research laboratory and the fertility clinic. Along with this has been a trajectory within the theological and general Christian literature to assert categorically that human life acquires full moral and theological value at fertilization (frequently referred to as "conception" in the writings of Christians), thereby proscribing any destruction or modification of embryos. This shift has been accompanied by a move out of what might be seen as the arcane world of theological debate into the intensely practical world of biomedical research. And for some this has become a matter so crucial that it is worth staking all in its defence; detractors have to be defeated at any cost.

As a biomedical scientist I find myself in the midst of this conflagration. In my view I cannot ignore the potential offered by studies of the human embryo, from observational studies to experimentation, from their relevance for clinical procedures such as IVF or PGD to ground-breaking genetic studies. For instance, as an anatomist, all the developmental knowledge of early human development (human embryology) I have ever learned was based on the study of catalogues of human embryos acquired over a period of many years. I could not have avoided that knowledge even if I had wished to do so.[1] In the face of far more recent studies, I have a range of options: to avoid contact with all or most of these developments, refuse to comment on them, or pretend they do not exist. But if I did, I would not be fulfilling my role as a biomedical scientist and bioethicist, let alone as a Christian commentator on highly contentious issues.

It is of course far too late for me now, since I have written extensively on these topics, from the status of the embryo to IVF/PGD and to research on human embryos and embryonic stem cells, and hence the die is cast.[2] But why have I been prepared to stick my neck out when I know doing so will mean I garner great opprobrium from some of my Christian colleagues? Is it worth it, or am I being a martyr for an unworthy cause? This chapter and the next will, I hope, provide some answers in this unsettling territory.

Protection of the fetus, and more recently the embryo, has been seen as the domain of pro-life forces. As I have argued elsewhere, I do not warm to labels, since these confine people to pre-ordained boxes, frequently with impregnable walls. Additionally, people can be consigned to boxes they do not wish to occupy and which may not fairly describe their position. Over against the pro-life camp is the pro-choice one, and the same strictures apply here. Although these two designations, pro-life and pro-choice, dominate debate on prenatal life, a moment's reflection is sufficient to highlight their inadequacy. Each represents one end of an ethical continuum, and so much of ethical, and I would suggest Christian, response lies somewhere between these extremes.

1. For a useful review see Yamada, Hill, and Takakua, "Human Embryology."
2. Jones, "Christian Responses to Challenging Developments in Biomedical Science," 137–58; Jones, "Responses to the Human Embryo and Embryonic Stem Cells;," 199–222; Jones, "An Exploration of Religiously-Based Opposition to Clinical and Scientific Interference with the Embryo," 169–88; Jones, *Manufacturing Humans*.

Ostensibly, prenatal life is championed by pro-life advocates who claim that all human life is created equal regardless of level of development, education, and degree of dependency. Therefore, it is argued, taking the life of a "preborn baby" is a violation of the fundamental right to life. This movement was birthed in the abortion wars of the 1970s, especially in the United States, although its claims are said to extend far beyond the unborn, to everyone in fact—preborn baby, the newborn, the elderly, and those with disabilities and special needs. In spite of these grandiose claims, it is difficult to escape the feeling that embryos and fetuses constitute the major, even if not the only, concern for many pro-life spokespeople. Over against this, pro-choice arguments usually appeal to the mother's right to bodily autonomy, and it is on this basis that abortion is generally regarded as morally permissible. Hence, to deny a woman an abortion is to deny her the right to bodily autonomy. In other words, the emphasis here is again on abortion, this time the mother's wishes to the exclusion of all others.

There are more sophisticated versions of these positions, since many people do weigh up the two claims. For instance, someone who is pro-choice can accept that a fetus has a right to life, but conclude that this right is outweighed by the mother's right to bodily autonomy. In the same way, someone who is pro-life can accept that a mother has a right to bodily autonomy but insist that this right is outweighed by the fetus' right to life. There are also moderate positions between the two extremes, although it is easy to argue that they involve a degree of inconsistency. However, these details do not concern me here, since I simply want to make two points. The first is that the pro-life/pro-choice distinction is driven by abortion, and that in practice once this division is accepted it pushes people into one of two camps. The second point is that, once the anti-abortion/pro-abortion distinction is accepted in these simplistic terms, it tends to get translated into two corresponding agenda concerning embryos: respectively, opposition to embryo research or advocacy for embryo research. I have never been comfortable with this rigid distinction and have aimed to follow a precarious and treacherous path in the middle, but erring towards allowing some research on embryos.

Into the Laboratory and Clinic

The drift from protection of the fetus to protection of the embryo came to light with the appearance of IVF in the 1970s and later with the derivation of embryonic stem cells (ESCs) from embryos in the early 2000s. Each in its way cast the spotlight onto embryos in the laboratory and onto the ways in which they could be used for purposes other than their own flourishing. They were seen by some as being sacrificed for the benefit of others, whether patients in IVF clinics or research.

The watershed year in reproductive technology was 1978, when the first baby was born following fertilization in the laboratory and therefore outside a woman's body. However, this was the culmination of a series of revolutionary steps that had taken place over a number of years in research laboratories using experimental animals followed by humans. The story of IVF is that of technology taking control of reproduction. In the absence of this control, IVF would never have opened the door to a range of technological inputs from intracytoplasmic sperm injection (ICSI) to PGD, and then farther into the future the derivation and use of ESCs and gene editing of the embryo (see below). Not one of these would have been possible in the absence of the ability to undertake research using human embryos. The living and maturing human embryo had become the focus of scientific analysis, and from this there would be no retreat. This opened the door to explorations of the embryo's characteristics, the complex interacting steps of its development, and the mistakes that sometimes occur to misalign these very precise steps. Opportunities were now afforded for understanding congenital abnormalities, and in the longer term for rectifying some of them.

A mere recital of these experimental openings is sufficient to throw light onto what has become an incipient antagonism between some Christian approaches and embryological science, if what passes as Christian is a decidedly protectionist form of the pro-life position. My interest as a scientist and Christian is to look closely at this stance, on the ground that describing and understanding the intricacies of embryonic development uncovers the wonders of God's magnificent creation. Why then would Christians not rejoice in the face of this staggering complexity that usually unfolds without a hitch? Why not marvel at the wonders enshrined in embryonic development in the same way as many are entranced by the wonders of the stars and galaxies in the universe, or at the latest steps in understanding black holes?

Enticing as these questions are, they encounter what for some is an immovable dogma, that fertilization marks the beginning of new human life and that embryonic life is inviolable and therefore has to be protected at all costs. Put this way, the conflict is obvious; any study of embryos is off the scientific agenda, regardless of what insights into God's creation or therapeutic opportunities it may offer. Research using human embryos is out of bounds, and if a consistent position is adopted, there is no place for IVF, since embryos were destroyed in developing the procedure and continue to be destroyed in maintaining media of the highest standards essential for clinical use.[3] Protection of human embryos has emerged as a litmus test of faithfulness as a Christian, leading to the stance that no studies that jeopardize their integrity are acceptable to Christians (strictly, this should read "theologically conservative Christians"). This has all the hallmarks of the now-discredited warfare between science and faith; for me, this is a retreat into the past; a sad reminder that this section of the scientific world is closed to many faithful Christians.

It fascinates me to reflect on the manner in which the conflict over abortion has been translated into conflict over the embryo. The desire to protect the fetus threatened with being aborted has been extended to protect the embryo at risk of being produced in a laboratory and destroyed during a clinical procedure (such as IVF) or, if surplus to clinical requirements, to be used for research/therapeutic purposes. With this move, the whole weight of ethical interest has shifted to fertilization/conception itself.

The major biological differences between the embryo and fetus have become secondary within theological ethical debate, even though for me as an anatomist they are crucial for an understanding of embryological development.[4] The distinction between destroying life as in abortion and producing life as in IVF has disappeared because destruction of embryos is equated with destruction of fetuses. The result has been to downgrade the significance of scientific input into ethical and theological analyses of prenatal existence. The controversies over abortion have been seamlessly transmuted into debate over the reproductive technologies. Consequently, destruction of the fetus and destruction of the embryo have been conflated and have become morally and theologically equivalent.

Absolute moral value has been bestowed upon all human life from fertilization onwards. Consequently, a one-hour zygote has the same moral and theological status as a three-month-old fetus, a three-year-old child, or a fifty-year-old adult. Hence, research on human embryos is considered unethical and theologically untenable because it is regarded by conservative thinkers as equivalent to aborting a fetus or killing a child/adult. On

3. Jones, "*In Vitro* Fertilization and the Destruction of Embryos," 163–74.
4. Jones and Telfer, "Before I was an Embryo, I was a Pre-Embryo: or Was I?" 32–49.

occasion even the word "murder" is used. Once absolute moral value is bestowed upon embryos and prenatal human life, it is a small step to regard embryos as sacrosanct.

The significance of this for biomedical scientists is immense because it closes the door to any investigations into the organization, development, and characteristics of human embryos. That may not concern either the general public or theologians, but from my perspective it is as significant as not being able to dissect and study the dead human body. The ability to do this was the result of a long-fought battle in Europe from the fourteenth to nineteenth centuries (chapter 2), and I sometimes wonder why it does not concern Christians today. The ability to study *in vitro* embryos (embryos in the laboratory) has much in common with this, even acknowledging the obvious differences. It is ironic that, prior to the 1960s, Christian thinkers showed very little interest in embryos, even though embryologists and reproductive biologists were gaining insights into them by studying historical catalogues of early human remains, such as the Carnegie embryo collection from the early 1900s, together with experimental animal embryos. All this changed with the advent of IVF as a clinical procedure in the late 1970s and into the 1980s. This was seen as a challenge of immense proportions to theological thinking, with its lack of signposts on how best to view these once-hidden entities. This was a new world for which Christian thinkers were ill-prepared, since the notion of the high moral status of the embryo, and its consequent inviolability, led to total rejection of any interference with human embryos. This immediately put many theologians, as well as large swathes of the conservative Christian community, at odds with the scientific community and unable to contribute productively to bioethical debate.[5]

The ground-breaking research in the United Kingdom that led to the successful development of IVF clinically was largely the work of Robert Edwards, a Cambridge physiologist, who relentlessly forged ahead with this work even though many around him viewed it as scientifically impossible and ethically untenable. He was his own man; a basic scientist who longed to understand human fertilization, an applied scientist who was driven to help those with infertility issues, and a controversialist who longed for meaningful ethical debate. He wanted to engage with politicians, philosophers, and theologians because he wanted society to take informed decisions.[6]

---

5. There are many examples, including Cameron, *Embryos and Ethics*; O'Donovan, *Begotten or Made?*

6. See Johnson, "Robert Edwards: The Path to IVF," 245–62.

These were his positive features, but he was frustrated by what he saw as the lack of interest in what he had set out to do. To make matters worse, he was provocative, and on occasion this proved an obstacle to positive engagement with others. Nevertheless, he had a profound understanding of the field, and he wrote extensively and perceptively about the ethical implications of his work. As he looked back much later, in 2007, he wrote that he and his team had been determined to achieve IVF as long as it did not result in damage to the resulting children. This is where his interests lay, and not on the loss of embryos that occurred during his formative studies. Hence, his starting point was quite different from that of many Christians writing on IVF a few years after the birth of the first individual by IVF. It is sad that theologians failed to interact with him when he was initially trying to map out the ethical implications of his work. He took the ethical dimensions of his work seriously even if his bias towards the legitimacy of what he was doing may have shone through too clearly.[7]

Unfortunately, he failed to interest Christian writers in what he was doing, even though everything was published in the scientific literature. It was not until the first IVF birth in 1978 and subsequent debate about this in the 1980s, by which time IVF had entered the medical mainstream, that religious authorities began to realize that reproduction may have changed forever and that embryos were threatened as they had become the center of scientific attention. The consensus of conservative Christian writers and thinkers was one of despair that a sacred line had already been crossed.

This is not the forum to follow subsequent developments in IVF and related technology, except to say that, as one should have expected, the score card has been mixed. The uses to which it has been put have reflected ongoing changes in the cultural mores of the societies in which it has been practiced, some of which have been distasteful to many Christians, in my opinion with some justification. The scene has also been muddied by the commercialization of the IVF "industry" and the lack of control over it in certain countries. All this is far removed from central Christian concerns and should not be used to reject outright any technological interference in the early stages of human life.

---

7. Edwards, "Reflections on Learning about Morals and Ethics in Biomedicine," 7–11.

At the Margins

Clearing the Way on Embryos and Beginnings

These technological and clinical developments eventually forced Christian thinkers to confront what was going on in early human development and with it the question of "when human life begins." This is often framed in very simple terms with the expectation of receiving a very simple answer. It is at point X or point Y. Before point X there is nothing, after point X there is everything. Or, alternatively, before point Y there is nothing of great moral concern; after point Y there is something of inestimable value. The pressure to give such an answer is usually immense, so much so that people feel aggrieved when they are not provided with one, even if it is an answer with which they can take issue. To refuse to answer such a simple question is seen as obfuscating, as being pig-headed, or the sad indecision of an impoverished thinker. Surely anyone in the business of ethics or moral theology has had time to formulate their position, which by definition will indicate a clear point of demarcation. And for scores of Christians the correct answer is fertilization.

This is not of mere theoretical interest, since human embryos have been available for study in the laboratory for over fifty years. As soon as this became feasible, they could be assessed for abnormalities and they could be used for research purposes. These developments indicate that what has become paramount is the status of the very early human embryo, especially the blastocyst (a fluid-filled entity at five to seven days after fertilization). These blastocysts contain an inner cell mass (ICM), some of the cells of which will ultimately give rise to the new individual, and external trophectoderm cells, which give rise to the future placenta and support tissues. The status of blastocysts is central to ethical debate, since they are capable of serving as a source of ESCs that are of interest due to their potential for contributing to the repair of adult tissues.

But we need to go further. When we ask the question, "When does human life begin?," what are we asking? Are we talking about a new human existence in the sense in which a new biological unit has come into play? In other words, is it the same as asking when does a new dog life begin for a dog or a new sheep life for a sheep? At the purely biological level, it is self-evident that a new human life begins once the process of fertilization has been completed, simply because that is the start of a whole host of processes that, given a supportive environment and minimal abnormalities, will terminate in an adult organism, whether this be human, dog, or sheep.

The Embryo, the Reproductive Technologies, and Christian Faithfulness

But this, taken in isolation of any other considerations, does not provide a very precise answer, because fertilization itself is a process incorporating a series of important steps. Even here there is a potential trap; development may not commence with fertilization but with somatic cell nuclear transfer (SCNT) or induced pluripotent stem cells (IPSCs—from adult tissue). Eventually a new individual may develop from an embryo-like entity that has never been fertilized using sperm and egg.

But is a biological answer the one most people are interested in? To this question there is a wide variety of answers, because what people like Christians and ethicists are generally concerned with is how much value or protection should be bestowed upon an embryo. This is the reason why a distinction between human life and personhood is frequently introduced, a distinction between "being human" (as with the biological definition) and "being a person" (when the biological entity should be valued as a human person). What this distinction signifies is that, with the recognition of personhood, an individual must be valued and protected exactly as all human persons should be valued and protected. By implication, there may be those who are human but who are not persons in the fullest sense, and therefore do not have the protection we normally expect to give to persons. Possibly early embryos fit into this category, especially early embryos in the laboratory.

This distinction horrifies some people on the ground that no human beings should ever be classed as non-persons. For some, not even a newly fertilized egg, let alone a human blastocyst, can be classed as a non-person. All are persons simply because they are human; no additional criteria are necessary. Hence, for many Christians, the distinction between humans as biological entities and humans as persons devalues human life, since a newly fertilized egg and a blastocyst are as morally significant as are any of us reading this book. They also fear that a distinction like this may lead to a situation whereby fetuses, those who are mentally disabled and the demented, will also be demoted to a non-personal status and will be regarded as disposable.

Some Christians also make the theological point that, since all humans are made in the image and likeness of God, it is not possible to conclude that one human is worth less than another human. This stems from the stance that every human being is made in the image of God (*imago dei*), bestowing upon every human life a unique dignity and unique value. In these terms, the earliest of embryos have precisely the same footing as every other human being. Therefore, since God loves all human beings, he also loves all embryos, leading to the conclusion that we must do the same. Hence, under no circumstances should research be conducted on any human embryos unless it is for the benefit of those particular embryos. Consequently, the argument goes, it is hypocritical to claim to love an embryo but then destroy it and others like it for research purposes. Where does this leave us? To answer this question, we need to return to blastocysts.

The World of Blastocysts

As with every issue in this early developmental area, these theological statements raise queries of their own. How do we know that God loves every embryo, and what does God's love for blastocysts actually mean? Did Christ die for every blastocyst, including the 70 percent of all blastocysts that are biologically incapable of developing beyond two to three weeks' gestation because of in-built abnormalities? What does it mean to state that God is imaged in every blastocyst, including those that will never develop beyond blastocysts?

On the surface, these questions give the appearance of being playthings of academics with nothing better to do than speculate about theoretical niceties. And yet, when confronted by decisions about undertaking IVF, carrying out PGD, or conducting research on human embryos, answers to such questions have to be given. For some people, it sounds shocking to suggest that blastocysts may not be the specific objects of God's love and may not be made in God's image. And yet, this is a daily issue for those working in fertility clinics, where decisions are being made about which embryos to implant in a woman undergoing IVF, those with a high chance of developing into a future individual (viable embryos) as opposed to those with a next-to-no chance of developing into a new individual (non-viable). If both groups are regarded as imaging God, is there a moral and spiritual obligation to implant non-viable as well as viable embryos, on the ground that this obligation entails doing everything possible to actualize the potential for life even when the possibility of success is exceedingly remote?

Although my emphasis has been on either-or perspectives, there are alternative positions that view embryos and fetuses as increasing in worth as biological and personal development unfolds and perhaps also growing into the image of God. Such positions attempt to take seriously the biological phenomena that characterize the growing embryo, including the emergence of well-defined biological organization and individuality, alongside a decrease in the potential for its cells to be redirected to form different tissues and organs. There is a sense of a "coming into being" as the developing entity moves along the continuum that marks embryonic development. These alternatives raise exceedingly important issues and encompass the whole range of positions one is likely to encounter, but they are no more than footnotes to my concerns in this chapter.

One of the characteristics of so much debate on the status of early embryos has been that they are usually viewed as isolated and essentially self-contained entities. Their status, whatever it may be, is inherent to them. They have this status regardless of where they are encountered—in a woman's uterine tubes, in a woman's uterus embedded in the uterine wall, in a woman's abdominal cavity (as in an ectopic pregnancy), in a Petri dish in the laboratory, or in a laboratory freezer. Some people regard all these, no matter what their location, as human persons, even though some of them lack the potential to become fully developed persons. In other words, this perspective takes no account of the embryo's environment. Neither does it take any account of the human community within which the embryos are encountered.

Blastocysts are found naturally, as well as artificially, in a range of environments, some of which enhance their development, whereas others hinder it. In other words, some blastocysts possess the inherent, as well as environmental, potential to become flourishing individuals; others lack this potential. While this is a biological observation, it has theological overtones. Does a blastocyst only image God if it is in a conducive environment? If we argue that a blastocyst with no potential for further development images God, we are in effect claiming that all human tissue images God. Is this what we mean to claim?

And then there are conflict situations, such as the choice between disposing of a surplus embryo in an IVF program, or using it for research or therapeutic purposes? Which is the better path? The frequently encountered response in Christian circles is that surplus embryos should never be produced, hence bypassing the conflict. While this represents one particular ideal, and a valid ideal at that, numerous surplus embryos exist in our societies. What is to be done with these embryos?

A frequently encountered riposte is that this is "cooperating with evil" by using "morally tainted" material. Expressions like these are usually encountered in dealing with the use of aborted tissue, such as with vaccines based, possibly, on cell lines such as HEK 293 (derived from human embryonic kidney cells grown in tissue culture taken from a female fetus) linked to an abortion many years ago (see chapter 4). The thrust of this criticism is that the postulated moral evil of the original abortion carries over to the vaccines based on this particular cell line.

This raises the concept of *moral complicity*, with its assertion that it is impossible to isolate the original maleficence from the subsequent good. The ethical decision in this instance is whether to accept or reject the notion of moral complicity, on condition that there is complete separation between the two acts. This involves weighing the good of lives saved by widespread use of a successful vaccine, against the evil outcomes of the original abortion. Account has to be taken of the human cost on both sides of the equation, a frequently encountered dilemma in medical ethics. And this surely is also a dilemma for Christians, since under other circumstances the saving of lives would be regarded as a good to be espoused. The dilemma in this case is not that of doing evil in order that good may be accomplished, since the evil (if that is what it is) has already been done and cannot be undone. Rather, it is the choice between refusing to save lives that could be saved, by producing and using an effective vaccine, against defending a theoretical absolute. There is no escape from compromise; the question is which compromise we are willing to make and which will best heighten the dignity of human lives.

Exploring Protectionist Stances among Christians

While there is a diversity of Christian stances on the moral standing of the human embryo, the fallback position is invariably a protectionist one. This is particularly the case in the more conservative Protestant circles, as well as in Roman Catholic ones. This stance signifies that protection is to extend from fertilization onwards. An example of this was provided by the statement of an *ad hoc* group of Christian theologians from the Anglican, Catholic, Orthodox and Reformed traditions in the United Kingdom, as they sought to respond to a House of Lords Select Committee on stem cell research in 2001. While the theologians involved came from a variety of religious traditions and theological persuasions, they put forward five principal considerations to inform any Christian evaluation of the moral status of the embryo. These included: "each human being is called and consecrated by God in the womb from the first moment of his or her existence, before he or she becomes aware of it. Traditionally, Christians have expressed the human need for redemption as extending from the moment of conception."[8]

This statement is expressed as the traditional Christian position, at least from the perspective of these major strands within the Christian church. It also refers to the need for redemption from conception onwards, even if the intent here is far from self-evident. Lying behind this position are the narratives of the Annunciation, the Visitation, and the Nativity, plus the parables of the good Samaritan and the sheep and the goats. In light of this position, all biomedical procedures should aim to protect embryos at risk of being destroyed. No alternative theological positions are floated, since an embryo-protection framework is accepted as foundational. Note that there is no reference to any scientific input.

Against such a staunch statement as this from a highly prestigious group of Christian theologians, there appears to be no room for any biomedical scientists, let alone Christian biomedical scientists. This is accentuated by a detailed examination of the status of the human embryo by another theologian, namely Calum MacKellar, in his 2017 book *The Image of God, Personhood and the Embryo*. His treatise is based on the thinking of an assemblage of highly reputable theologians through the ages. What emerges is a stark divide between one strand of theological thinking on prenatal human life and the thinking and approach of most embryologists and developmental scientists.

The fulcrum of his thinking is that each new embryo is a creation of God and an expression of profound and real love. Consequently, there is never a moment in the existence of a child when they are not loved by God. This love applies no matter how the embryo came into existence—through rape or incest, or within a happy family, nor its location in the uterus, the abdominal cavity, or *in vitro* in the laboratory. God's love applies irrespective of whether or not they possess the capability of developing into a child.

This theological analysis is all-encompassing, leaving no place for any biological insights. "From a theological perspective . . . The number of cells or their state of differentiation in a person may not actually matter . . . it is whether the embryo exists, is complete and is a whole that is important."[9] The conclusion is that the embryo has full moral status no matter where it is found and regardless of whether or not it has any potential, biologically and

---

8. Jones et al., "A Theologian's Brief on the Place of the Human Embryo within the Christian Tradition, and the Theological Principles for Evaluating its Moral Status."

9. MacKellar, *The Image of God, Personhood and the Embryo*, 201.

environmentally, to develop any farther. Embryonic existence for as little as a few seconds is what counts. Biology has become irrelevant, meaning that there is no room for the contribution of a biomedical scientist or reproductive biologist, whether Christian or not.

Similar conclusions are found in the official Roman Catholic position on IVF as laid out in *Donum Vitae* in 1987, which gave unconditional respect to developing human life from "the moment of conception." This led to the early embryo (zygote) being considered inviolable, and to condemnation of any destruction of *in vitro* human embryos for research purposes. This was because, by choosing certain embryos to live and others to die, researchers are usurping the place of God. By opening up these processes to human decision-making, it leads to technological domination over the origin and destiny of the human person and amounts to what the document names as "radical eugenics." Inevitably, all the artificial reproductive technologies (ARTs) including IVF become unworthy means of bringing human life into existence and making babies born via IVF into products of human ingenuity.[10]

In order to update this advice and reaffirm the dignity of the human embryo from conception onwards, *Dignitas Personae* appeared in 2008. In this, the official Roman Catholic position formulated objections to all procedures associated with IVF on the basis that embryos are sacrosanct.[11] Consequently, there is no place for any human control over the reproductive process. The one object of moral and theological concern is the embryo, as opposed to concerns stemming from infertility issues, the health of a marriage, or the welfare of the prospective child. Interestingly, not all Roman Catholic ethicists agree, with some emphasizing embryological data, the role of prudence, and an ethic of feminist care, while others reject what they view as an outdated physicalist version of natural law and excessive fears about a eugenic mentality. The latter pay attention to scientific data and social conditions, unlike the Vatican statements.

Protestant input stems from the 1970s and 1980s. A notable contributor was Paul Ramsey, an American Presbyterian ethicist, who wrote eloquently about the reproductive technologies in the 1970s, when he was practically a lone voice speaking out of the religious establishment.[12] He

---

10. Congregation for the Doctrine of the Faith, "Instruction on Respect for Human Life in its Origin and on the Dignity of Procreation Replies to Certain Questions of the Day."

11. Congregation for the Doctrine of the Faith, "*Instruction Dignitas Personae* on Certain Bioethical Questions."

12 Ramsay, *Fabricated Man*; Ramsay, "Shall We Reproduce? 1 and 2."

was driven by the fear that fetuses and subsequent children resulting from IVF would be harmed in the process. He was also troubled by the thought that the increasing power of scientific manipulation would threaten the role of God in upholding and sustaining human beings through illness and infirmity. Interestingly, Ramsey paid limited attention to the embryo, although he was writing before the birth of the first IVF individual.

I have always been encouraged by Ramsey's writings. While I deviate from some of his conclusions, he was correct in asserting that reliance on the artificial would increase markedly once IVF became socially acceptable. He was also correct in speculating that humans would come to look more to science than to God in the reproductive area. These are salutary reminders of the misleading power of technological directions in the absence of social and theological input to balance undue reliance upon the artificial.

Searching for Theological Answers

Against this barrage of assertions from leading theologians, how can I, a mere anatomist, have anything to say? This is a crucial question, since I take seriously the expertise of those with theological insights that I lack. Should I simply accept that there is no place for the perspectives of Christians who are biomedical scientists and that whatever conclusions biomedical scientists come to will be unacceptable to Christians? And yet I do not feel I can remain silent, since there must be some way in which the biomedical sciences can have an input into theological thinking. Surely, they must throw some light onto God's world, and on the way in which the human embryo develops to become what ultimately is that wonderful creation that we recognize as a human being. The gradual unfolding of each individual human being is a manifestation of God's amazing design and direction, the details of which are revealed by biomedical science. Christians should rejoice in the face of such profound understanding.

The dominant clinching argument put forward by many Christians when thinking about the embryo is that human life is sacred from conception. Two claims are made here. First, that human life is sacred, and second, that this sacredness is conferred at conception. Both claims are frequently taken to be implicit in Scripture. On the basis that all human life is sacred, many Christian thinkers have argued for an ethics of life that precludes abortion, infanticide, mercy killing, suicide, capital punishment, and the destruction of human lives generally. One notable exception is war.

However, the sanctity of human life is rarely defined. Its religious basis is apparent, since "sanctity" literally means "holiness." A strong interpretation points to the inviolability of human life, according to which no human life, from the earliest embryonic stages, can be taken by other human beings under any circumstance whatsoever. A weaker interpretation points to a reverence for human life that is regarded as having a value inherent within itself and that is to be cared for and protected as much as possible.

Surprisingly, perhaps, the term "sanctity of human life" does not appear explicitly in Scripture. Human life is never said to be "holy" in the way that the Sabbath or God himself are said to be holy. In spite of this, some Christian writers find an indirect basis for the concept in Scripture. For instance, God created humans in his own image (Gen 1:26–27), something that does not apply to other forms of life. The murder of other humans is proscribed (Gen 9:6; Exod 20:13; 1 John 3:12,15), and the incarnation of Jesus in which God took on human form points to the profound significance of humanity in God's sight. Further evidence in favor of a privileged status for human beings is the notion that human life is to be viewed as a gift held in trusteeship (1 Cor 6:19b–20), and that our bodies as Christians are temples of the Holy Spirit (1 Cor 6:19).

These are very important concepts for the ethical life. But this is the furthest we can go, and whether they add up to the sacredness of human life is open to debate. An unfortunate tendency by some has been to make the sanctity of human life into an absolute value that trumps all others and brings ethical debate to a close. I sometimes get the impression that in the eyes of some it has almost acquired the standing of an idol. This approach comes out particularly in connection with abortion and other reproductive issues but is resorted to far less vigorously in other areas where lives are also at stake. Neither is it of more than limited relevance when confronted by borderline cases. This is because it is of little assistance when one "sacred" life is pitted against another "sacred" life, or the interests of one individual or group are pitted against the interests of another individual or group. Resolution of dilemmas of this nature entails treating some sacred objects as more sacred than other sacred objects.

The accompanying clinching argument is that human life begins at conception. It is frequently argued that there is support in the Bible for this position. Women are referred to as conceiving, but the writers of the time knew nothing about conception or fertilization in the way in which we do. The Hebrew and Greek phrases translated as "conceived" ought to be rendered "become pregnant." While much was known about pregnancy, and about the growth of the unborn "child," we do not know whether the unborn were thought of as persons in anything like a modern sense. Two examples occur in Job 10:10 and Psalm 139:13–16, both of which are poetic and powerful. But do they tell us anything about what the writers thought was actually happening inside the womb? They would never have seen inside the body any more than anatomists would have seen inside the body until the early beginnings of human dissection as we know it in the fourteenth century—with one or two isolated examples much earlier (chapter 2). As far as we can ascertain, the biblical writers viewed the unborn as developing from something formless into something developed and complete. It is also very clear that both the psalmist and Job believed that God was intimately involved in these processes.

The biblical writers could never have given specific answers to the type of questions with which we are confronted. The Bible does not specifically map out the significance of fertilization any more than it maps out the significance of blastocysts in the laboratory. Nevertheless, there are general principles that stem in large part from the incarnation, when Jesus revealed the image of God in human form and thereby demonstrated the importance of bodily existence. These principles lay the groundwork for our thinking about human beings, namely, that they are created in God's image, are precious to God, have a special status, are to be treated with dignity because this stems from God's love and concern for them, and are to be respected.

General as these themes are, they are foundational, since they constitute important guideposts for all our thinking about ways in which human beings are to be treated. They impart to all humans a splendor and significance that we dare not overlook, whether this be in reproductive ethics, numerous aspects of social policy, or international relations. They point towards equality, compassion, and protection as opposed to inequality, exploitation, and social programming. But where does this leave life before birth?

References to prenatal human existence are encountered in passages such as Job 10:3–12, Psalm 139:13–16, Isaiah 49:1, Jeremiah 1:5, and Luke 1:41–44, where prenatal humans emerge as part of the human community and therefore are to be viewed as special to us and to God. Human life is also referred to as a gift of God (Gen 4:1; 16:2; 29:31, 32; 30:22, 23; Ruth 4:13). These passages reveal the testimonies of a very small number of people about the ways in which God had led them and looked after them.

They are personal and private confessions about God and his purposes for them. They are far removed from the aseptic, clinical world of the reproductive technologies or the equally aseptic world of academic discussions on the moral status of embryos and fetuses. The closest we come to this today are individuals testifying to God's dealings with them throughout their lives—exact parallels to some of these Old Testament confessions. These biblical passages touching on prenatal life are confessions about God and his purposes.

It is in this sense that my life is a gift from God; I am grateful to God for the gift of human life and the opportunity for me to experience all that human life has to offer. As I look back, I am able to exclaim that God has protected me throughout the whole of my physical existence—from the earliest stages of gestation through to the present day. However, enormous care has to be exercised in moving from such important theological statements about me and my life to contemporary reproductive issues of what can and cannot be done in laboratories and clinics. The worlds and the interests are quite different. For instance, what does it mean for me to claim that God knew me before my genetic blueprint was in place, before there was even the merest hint that an individual with my genetic characteristics would be born? In no sense is it meaningful to talk about God's purposes for me two hundred years before I came into existence. This is not to deny that God may have known me well before I ever came to be, nor that he has had purposes for my life, but it is presumptuous to link these to any specific genetic, let alone epigenetic, features that have laid the basis for what I am as a biological individual.

Consequently, the move from such personal expressions of praise by God's people to an understanding of how God views all embryos and fetuses represents a seismic shift from the particular to the general, from confessions about God's activities in the lives of particular individuals to statements about how everyone should view embryos *en masse*. In my estimation God's protection of the embryo that was to become David (Ps 139:13–16) does not justify the assertion that he expects contemporary societies to protect every embryo brought into existence. The ethical question is whether all these embryos should be produced in the first place, what are the reasons for doing this, and how will they be used once produced? But a similar set of considerations applies to giving birth to children.

The furthest I consider we can go is to state that God is concerned about embryos and fetuses, just as he is concerned about all human life after birth. This is where the general principles of special status, dignity, and respect enter the picture. What this leads to is serious commitment to the welfare of embryos and fetuses. While this may sound uninteresting, it ensures that we never treat human life before birth frivolously and that we never underestimate the worth of those who may be like us in the future. The population of embryos is an important population, just as is the postnatal population. We are to extend neighbor love to prenatal human life, and we are to value prenatal human life.

In deciding what can or cannot be done to and with embryos, it is the nature of the decision-making that is crucial. The choices are serious clinical choices, between blastocysts capable of developing further and those incapable of doing so, between blastocysts that will likely develop into healthy individuals and those that will not. Even the use of blastocysts in research should be governed by a serious therapeutic rationale and the well-grounded hope that it will lead to an improvement in the welfare of individuals and the community in the future.

It is also important that we make explicit the implications of what it is we are doing. If human embryos are destroyed, either clinically or in research, the assumption is being made that these particular embryos are not made in the image of God and that God does not have a special love for them. If this assumption is incorrect, we should not be doing what we are doing. However, this is far from a novel situation, since numerous human embryos are lost in all forms of reproduction, very often due to genetic and chromosomal abnormalities. And in practice it is the embryos that go on to become babies and individuals like us that we most revere, and not the extremely early embryos that (unknowingly) succumb.

What is important is what kind of people we are. What is our moral commitment to others, including all those who are not quite like us, and how do we recognize the human face in others? This will not provide us with neat ethical or theological answers, but it does frame the ethical debate and the hard thinking involved in this. It also forces us to hold the demands that embryos make on us alongside the demands that all other human beings make on us. If we contend that all human beings have a dignity bestowed upon them by God, we are compelled to uphold their dignity and wellbeing as much as we can, realizing that there are circumstances where conflicts will arise between one postnatal human being and another and between one postnatal human being and a prenatal human being. Welcome to the messiness of ethical decision-making. Thankfully, there is guidance, including theological guidance, available.

7

Biomedical Technology, Christian Thinking, and the Public Square

Personal Involvement in Decisions on Embryo Research

FOR A NUMBER OF years, I was on the New Zealand governmental advisory committee to the minister of health on assisted reproductive technologies (ACART). While ACART had responsibility for overseeing the whole gamut of the ARTs, much of the debate when I was a member revolved around whether or not research could be undertaken on human embryos. The New Zealand stance on this was (and still is) unusual in that procedures such as IVF and PGD, which entail the destruction of embryos, are sanctioned, and yet research cannot be conducted on human embryos superfluous to the requirements of those undergoing IVF. The act under which ACART functions allows for this up to fourteen days gestation, on one condition: that the minister of health gives permission for ACART to proceed to draw up guidelines. Starting in 2007, no minister was prepared to allow ACART to draw up such guidelines; this continued until the early part of 2022, meaning that research on viable human embryos has remained in limbo for over fifteen years.

This position satisfies no one. For those who would opt for a very restrictive regime, this is nothing more than a Pyrrhic victory, since the situation depends upon the dictate of one individual politician, the minister of health. Embryo research is not prohibited and yet cannot be carried out. For users of fertility services, this is a negative outcome, since it closes the door to the option of donating their surplus embryos for research purposes. Their only options are donation to another couple or discarding them. For those opposed to research on embryos, the situation could change at any point if a minister gives the go-ahead for guidelines to be drawn up.[1]

As a member of ACART, I found myself in the middle of this ongoing debate on embryo research. This presented me with two sets of issues. The immediate one as a committee member was the ethical inconsistency of the country's position on embryo destruction. The second was my stance as a Christian and whether I was prepared to support undertaking research on human embryos. I shall deal first with what I regarded as my responsibility as an ethical commentator in the public domain.

The Bioethical Debate

From the 1980s onwards, the ethical literature falls into two clearly delineated responses to IVF: the negative, with its suspicion of IVF and in some cases its rejection; and the positive, with its stress on the needs of the infertile and consequent acceptance of IVF. Those who are negative towards IVF pay particular attention to protection of the embryo, in contrast to those who are positive, where the emphasis is on the needs of the infertile.[2]

Within a pluralist society, a balance has to be found between these two positions, since each represents different and, in this case, incompatible conceptions of the good. The aim of public policy is to reflect neither extreme to the exclusion of the other. However, there is no escape from competing interests: those intent on protecting embryos, those seeking to overcome infertility problems and those wishing to address genetic- and chromosomally-based illnesses in their families.

IVF is a clinical procedure that has to be practiced according to the most rigorous biomedical and clinical standards in operation, standards that depend in part on the latest research on the best available laboratory conditions for the health of the embryos that will be implanted into a woman. Since the hoped-for end result is a living child, that child's well-being is dependent upon the health of the embryo. This necessitates ongoing research that inevitably involves research on human embryos. When this

---

1. For further details, see my chapter on "The Political Debate on Embryo Research in New Zealand and the Role of Religious Actors and Arguments."

2. Jones, "Where Does New Zealand Stand on Permitting Research on Human Embryos?"

research cannot be undertaken in one country (New Zealand in this instance), it becomes dependent upon research conducted in other countries.

As I thought about these issues, I came to realize that there are four possible models of embryo protection. Model 1 is protection of the embryo and rejection of embryo research and all procedures connected with it, including IVF and PGD. Model 2 is acceptance of existing policies in New Zealand, that is, rejection of embryo research in the present, but acceptance of IVF and PGD. Model 3 is acceptance of embryo research outside New Zealand, its rejection in New Zealand, but accepting modifications based on data from research carried out in other countries. This leaves model 4, the most liberal, with its acceptance of embryo research.

Of these models, 1 and 4 are consistent in their stances, prohibition in model 1 and permission in model 4. The two intervening models (2 and 3) are less consistent in that they accept to differing degrees the results of research on embryos, either in the past and/or on a continuing basis. While they aim to protect embryos in the future, they are prepared to benefit from data and procedures obtained from embryo destruction in the past (and possibly in the present in other countries).

I found the two intermediate models (2 and 3) very difficult to accept on account of their inconsistency. As a society we either aim to protect human embryos or we do not. This forces us to ask on what grounds it can be acceptable to destroy (or allow to perish) embryos surplus to the requirements of a clinical fertility program, but refuse to allow use of these about-to-be-destroyed embryos for research aimed at contributing to an understanding of the causes of infertility. For me, a society that allows IVF also has a duty to be involved in ongoing research that will increase the efficacy and safety of the procedures being used. Without this, one is entirely dependent upon research carried out elsewhere that by one's own definition is unethical.

This brings us back to the two contrasting but consistent models, no destruction of embryos (their protection and no IVF), or the acceptance that embryos can be destroyed under well-defined conditions with the aim of benefitting families and children. This contrast may appear overly simplistic, and it does ignore some of the possibilities, and yet it lays out realistically the options and the consequences. The dilemma for those Christians who regard all embryos as being sacrosanct, and therefore never to be destroyed, is obvious: IVF is unacceptable ethically and I imagine theologically. As a member of ACART I had to think of the pluralist society to which I belong and of the very diverse views on the status of the embryo across society. In the eyes of some Christians this will have placed me in an untenable position, representing as it does a compromise between two extremes. I was poignantly aware of this, but considered that it represented an outworking of the nuanced position I had arrived at as a Christian on the embryo and its relationships within the human community (see below).

Acceptance of IVF by a society alters the context for approaching the protection of embryos. This is because research using embryos is intimately woven throughout every aspect of IVF. The destruction of embryos will occur regardless of whether any research will be carried out on surplus embryos. There will, almost inevitably, be embryos surplus to clinical requirements, that if not used by other couples in an IVF program (so-called pre-natal adoption) have no future as viable human beings. Christians are free to reject such an outcome, but in order to be ethically consistent, that means rejection of IVF.[3]

I argue that a society that allows IVF also has a duty to be involved in ongoing research that will increase the efficacy and safety of the procedures being used. Without this, one is entirely dependent upon research carried out in other countries, regardless of the ethical standards applying in those countries. This is a medical ethical issue for the profession and society. The relationship between embryos and future children is an intimate one whenever the existence of the latter depends upon a technological procedure like IVF. Without IVF they would not exist; with it, not only do they exist but many aspects of their health and well-being depend upon the protocols employed in the clinic.

Contributing as a Christian

Up to this point I have worn my bioethical hat, with minimal reference to Christian input. Of course, there is no way in which I wish to compartmentalize my attitudes into secular bioethical ones on the one hand and spiritual on the other. I have no intention of agreeing to embryo research as an academic commentator and rejecting it as a Christian within church circles. In both contexts I am one and the same individual. And this is where Christians, such as myself, sometimes get into difficulties within their church communities. If I insist on functioning within the secular-pluralist space, and I regard this as my calling, I have to walk in territory that will

3. Jones, "*In Vitro* Fertilization and the Destruction of Embryos," 163–74.

be uncomfortable for a good number of my fellow believers. And some of these may reject my contribution for this reason. This is why science-faith questions in the biomedical sphere pose challenges today that are rarely encountered in, say, the physical sciences. It is one thing to advocate idealistic positions within church circles, where you are speaking to the faithful who do not have to face any of the medical or research questions facing biomedical scientists and practitioners. It is quite different walking the narrow bridge between the church and surrounding society, where those with fertility problems are calling out for assistance. Christian professionals do not have to accede to such demands, but they have to confront them with integrity and honesty.

Of course, I could have resigned from the committee or remained on it but argued against any hint of research on embryos. I could have put in a minority report and made my opposition eminently clear. I could also have stated that this was on the basis of my Christian faith. But had I done this, there would still have been the elephant in the room—the existence of IVF and my implicit acceptance of this with its built-in destruction of embryos. I imagine that if I held the position that no embryo should ever be intentionally destroyed, I would have had to walk away from any involvement in decision-making in the public square and indeed from any involvement in the embryological and reproductive side of anatomy.

This truly is a question of how Christians are to function on the frontline. Without advocating for any particular stance, various models present themselves. One is the witness/martyr one: stand up against what you regard as the major secularizing forces in society and do this in the name of Christ. In other words, oppose new developments as a Christian. The result is withdrawal from all ongoing debate and retreat from these and related technological developments. That has not been my position, and for some Christians it demonstrates my unfaithfulness as a Christian. For me, being immersed in the battle by bringing to the table the values I regard as enshrined in the Christian faith has been crucial. This may not have the glamour of standing valiantly for the faith, but it ensures that values pointing towards human dignity for all parties are brought to the fore. This in my estimation is a vital part of Christian witness within a pluralist environment.

Theology, Science, and the Public Square

As a scientist, the overwhelming message to emerge from the theological contributions I summarized in chapter 6 is a negative one (see *Exploring Protectionist Stances among Christians*, 106–9). It is that theology has all the answers Christians need when considering embryos and procedures impinging on them. There is no place for any scientific insights. Theology trumps science, leaving no place for any contribution by scientists who are Christians. If the embryo is inviolable, no investigations on it are acceptable, and Christians should leave well alone. According to this scenario, all embryological knowledge should be obtained from research on non-humans, assuming that research on experimental animal models is approved on scriptural grounds. Interestingly, there is very limited debate within conservative Christian circles on the legitimacy of research using animals.

If one believes that all truth is God's truth and that this is God's world that can be explored and understood using scientific means, this raises an interesting predicament. All aspects of early human development appear to have become exceptions and to be beyond exploration. In stating this I am not advocating that all forms of research on early humans, whether embryos or fetuses, can be justified, any more than such a *laissez faire* doctrine applies anywhere else. But I am perplexed that they are being placed totally out-of-bounds, in contrast to research on other humans or human tissue that is not generally considered totally out-of-bounds.

I have emphasized MacKellar's contribution because it is so thoroughly worked out and is so theologically explicit. For this I am deeply grateful to him. It demonstrates very convincingly that a prohibitionist theological position is as much anti-IVF as it is anti-abortion. The production of spare embryos in IVF is categorically rejected, as is PGD with its selection of embryos; and no genetic analysis is to take place that might lead to selecting one embryo over another. It follows that there can be no genetic manipulation of embryos and no gene editing, regardless of their goal. Some Christian commentators reject research on non-viable embryos that, by definition, are incapable of developing beyond a few days. This is because all are regarded as having the same value in God's sight, alive or dead. By this rationale no research would be allowed on dead adult humans, since they too are valuable in God's sight. The discussion becomes even more fraught when research on human embryos is expressed in emotive terms, as when it is likened to the human sacrifice of children.

Conclusions like these ignore the prenatal environment, suggesting there are no theological perspectives available on this environment. This is hardly surprising, since this would have been unknown territory to the biblical writers and church fathers. Current understanding is a product of embryological work spanning many decades. When theological explanations shun interdisciplinary dialogue, they become isolationist, meaning that embryos are placed beyond the reach of the human community and are seen as untouchable in a way foreign to all other members of the human community. By stressing the extreme vulnerability of embryos and their need for total protection, they have been placed beyond the reach of those who are capable of contributing to their future welfare.

As I view a position such as this one, my immediate response is to ask how practical it is. Undoubtedly, I respond in this manner because I am a scientist who is used to walking in a world dominated by practical concerns and conflicted tensions. I am also used to high-level administration where committee decisions are frequently compromises, the best that can be obtained in the circumstances. This is the world of pragmatic reality, which is often murky and far from the ideal. I have no problem with walking in territory like this, whereas others do. It is for me to appreciate where others are coming from and attempt to view the world through their eyes. As a Christian it is not for me to judge others who do not see the world through my eyes, although I do understand that we are all broken people, both in our actions and thinking. So often the ideal is unattainable; we do not live in a perfect sinless milieu, and we have to learn how best to inject into this ecosystem that which is closest to the ideal.

The role of compromise within Christian thinking and attitudes takes me into theological territory where I do not claim expertise. I look at the manner in which in the Old Testament God accepted procedures wanted by the Israelites that he knew would not be for their best. An example was their longing for a king, something he gave them in spite of knowing it would be disastrous. Moses allowed divorce because of the hardness of their hearts. Jesus recognized the latter, even though this was breaking the lifelong commitment of the marital bond. The woman taken in adultery was not stoned to death, but Jesus told her to go and sin no more. In all these instances, there was recognition that they were far from God's ideal pattern, but there was also recognition that God would work with and through these suboptimal patterns.

IVF and the Destruction of Embryos

With these thoughts in mind let me return to IVF and the loss of embryos. Is IVF possible without the loss of at least some embryos? Some Christian commentators have recognized the relationship between IVF and the loss of embryos, and a small number oppose the practice of IVF on these grounds. However, more are prepared to accept IVF on condition that no surplus embryos are produced, or if they are, all should be implanted into a woman. In other words, none should be left over and subsequently destroyed. Few commentators arguing in this way appear to realize that many embryos were destroyed during the development of these procedures, nor that ongoing research is required to ensure that the *in vitro* aspects of keeping embryos alive and healthy in the laboratory have to be constantly monitored. If embryos should never be intentionally destroyed, IVF in all its guises is morally tainted with evil.

In spite of these considerations, many conservative Christians are more positively disposed towards IVF than they are towards abortion or the production of ESCs. The perceived importance of families and family life helps to paint IVF in a relatively positive light despite compromises over the sanctity of embryos. The inconsistency of this position has been noted by some observers, especially in thinking about the acceptability or unacceptability of conducting research on embryos. Put simply, one might expect that anyone who permits couples to create multiple embryos for reproductive purposes would also, in principle, be prepared to allow scientists to undertake research on embryos no longer required for reproductive purposes. The goal of such research is to improve IVF as a clinical procedure. In practice, though, this is a step too far for many, who want to ensure that no embryos are "left over" by suggesting that all excess embryos are implanted into the woman concerned. Unfortunately, this raises a host of clinical and ethical problems, including the almost inevitable loss of some of the transferred embryos and the negative effects of multiple births on the health of the resulting children. Overlooking these fails to confront the nuances of serious ethical decision-making and the possibility that our actions may on occasion be morally troubling but still justifiable in the context of current clinical understanding.

The Christian Medical and Dental Associations (CMDA) in the United States confronts this tension in an exemplary manner, even if in my eyes it does not resolve it. CMDA accepts that many of the ARTs may be an appropriate expression of humankind's God-given creativity and stewardship under certain circumstances. Adopting a precautionary stance along these lines leads to the view that a number of procedures are inconsistent with God's design for the family, including: discarding or destroying embryos, the uterine transfer of an excess number of embryos, experimentation that involves embryo destruction, and any form of PGD that is carried out with the intention of discarding or destroying embryos.

Attempting to remain faithful to the premise that individual moral value commences at fertilization, the CMDA wants to limit the loss of embryos in IVF to no more than that encountered in natural fertilization. Since as many as 70 percent of embryos may be lost naturally, this provides a ball-park figure for the loss that can be morally accepted in IVF. This is different from rejecting any loss, because in practice if, say, twelve embryos are produced following ovarian stimulation, with three lost following embryo transfer, and a further two leading to successful pregnancies, the seven embryos left over equate with an embryo loss of around 60 percent.

This calculation sounds heartless and appears at odds with a protectionist stance on the embryo. In practice it probably finds little support among those intent on protecting the embryo under all circumstances. More to the point, it highlights the enormous obstacles to accepting IVF or any of the reproductive technologies for those determined to protect every embryo. This does not amount to rejection of that stance, but it serves to place it within a broad applied context.

Others with a protectionist stance towards embryos but realizing the practical ramifications of an unyielding idealist position reluctantly accept compromises. Even accepting that there should be no separation between sexual intercourse and procreation, some will consent when the separation necessitated by IVF is used to assist an infertile couple to have a child genetically related to them. The logic here is that this is bringing together what the fall has separated, even if remaining troubled by the intrusive nature of IVF, the production of spare embryos, and its dependence upon many years of embryo research. This is a nuanced and human response to a taxing situation, even as it reluctantly accepts that embryos were destroyed in the early stages of the development of IVF and its ongoing clinical modifications. In my view far more attention should be given to the theological underpinnings of this compromise, one that is encountered frequently when confronted with emotive ethical dilemmas. It brings out the contrast between idealism and realism, the realism in this instance being that, in nature, embryos are far from sacrosanct. Here they are glaringly dispensable, with numerous embryos routinely being lost in bringing each new individual into existence. This does not mean we are free to do what we like with them, but it is a salutary reminder of the fragility of embryos far away from the intrusions of technology.

A degree of positivity toward scientific and technological innovations in the reproductive area inevitably means being prepared to acknowledge that it is acceptable to destroy embryos under certain circumstances and to encourage research on (surplus) embryos. This in turn acknowledges the role of science in alleviating disease and in rectifying what may have gone amiss during development. The degree to which individuals and groups are prepared to go in this direction will differ, but compromises will be made in all cases.

The driving impetus is to ask what might be most pleasing to God. Phrasing the predicament in this manner points to the centrality of Christ and to biblical directives emphasizing humility, an ethic of responsibility, and stewardship of God's creation. It demands a close examination of one's motives in wanting a genetically related child of one's own as opposed to remaining childless, wanting a child without a genetically debilitating condition, fostering children, or adopting children in dire need.

The welfare of families, family relationships, and individuals should be central, stressing the significance of marriage. This is central to Christian life in society, since it throws the focus onto the significance of humans in the eyes of God—as his beings and, for Christians, as his people. Whatever limits are imposed flow from this framework. The welfare of embryos will not be ignored, but they are no longer the only consideration.

The way in which IVF has become a massive commercial venture in the years since its inception raises different issues. The original intention on the part of Robert Edwards was to provide a means by which infertile couples could have children of their own; this now sounds almost naïve. Of course, it still applies, but many forces have pushed it far beyond the bounds of a married heterosexual couple seeking a child of their own into a technological means of allowing almost anyone have a child—single women (or men), gay couples, women beyond reproductive age and even beyond menopause, and by using the donated gametes of a surrogate. The possibilities continue to "blossom," which is perhaps an unfortunate term to use here. In other words, IVF has become an industry driven by high costs and successful business ventures and paying little regard to any moral foundations beyond the whim of the consumer.

In the midst of this rampant commercialization of the reproductive technologies the well-being of the embryo is inevitably lost. For someone with my stance on the embryo this represents a sad transformation of what commenced with commendable goals, even if some of these were tarnished. My experience in New Zealand is that public policy with considerable governmental control can ensure that the reproductive technologies are not a Wild West, even if that is not the case in many other countries. Once more, this is where balance and control are essential if there is to be as much protection for embryos and women as possible.

A rejoinder to this turn of events is to claim that none of the ARTs should have been allowed in the first place. The same can be said of numerous developments to which we have become accustomed—from the motor car to nuclear fission, from air travel to the internet, from pesticides to mood-enhancing drugs. All have their uses and all have been sullied by misuse and abuse in practice. Christians, like everyone else, are called to act responsibly by weighing up as best they can that what they participate in will be God-honoring. It is here that the hard theological and ethical work begins. On the other hand, to reject outright certain procedures on the ground that they can be misused but accept others equally capable of being misused is less than responsible as beings created in the image of God.

Implications for the Public Square—Case Studies

This willingness to balance idealism and realism opens the way to dialogue with others in the public square, a dilemma that has arisen repeatedly with debate around reproductive technologies, especially embryo research and ESCs. This has come into prominence whenever there is political debate on legislation to allow and oversee research techniques involving embryos. A prominent case study was in the United States in 2001 when the then-president, George W. Bush, entered the debate by imposing a ban on federal funding for research on newly created ESC lines. Coming from a protectionist position, he was faced with a dilemma: to forbid any use of ESC lines, a stance that would have flowed from his ethical position, or allow limited use of existing cell lines. The policy to emerge was an uneasy compromise in that it confined the use of ESCs to those currently in existence but prohibited any further extraction of new cells. The goal was an understandable one: the protection of embryos while at the same time attempting to support some limited ESC research. In practice, it turned out to be a very unsatisfactory compromise both ethically and scientifically. Unfortunately, it failed to satisfy either side; it was a political construct with a questionable ethical basis. Undoubtedly, it was a genuine attempt to satisfy two conflicting interests, but it demonstrated that this sort of ethical compromise that fails to take account of scientific reality is bound to fail. Research on embryos is either accepted or it is rejected; it is very difficult, if not impossible, to find a position that both accepts and rejects this research.

I have touched on my membership of ACART, the government body in New Zealand with responsibility for advising the Minister of Health on policy issues covering an array of reproductive technologies. When inviting submissions from the general public on the prospect of allowing research on embryos surplus to the needs of those undergoing IVF, the committee was provided with a host of insights.

It soon emerged that much of the public opposition to embryo destruction has a religious base, even if it was not always made explicit. Repeatedly, embryo research involving embryo destruction was condemned on grounds that it was "playing God." Religiously-based responses frequently employed this language without explaining why "playing God" is to be decried or even what it means. For instance, one pro-life organization objected on the basis that human life begins at conception, claiming that this point signifies the time when the embryo is endowed by its creator with human rights. Since every embryo is regarded as a miracle of God's loving creation, its destruction was characterized as being akin to murder, since these were innocent and defenceless children. The religious language was very familiar to those making such claims, but far less so to members of the committee. What were they to make of repeated references to God and his love, and to the repeated claims that "human life begins at conception"? The terminology was foreign to some members of the committee, and the lack of adequate framing of these opinions within a meaningful scientific and clinical context proved problematic.[4]

Besides these non-negotiable positions, there were other more nuanced protectionist positions within religious contributions. For instance, one organization recognized that embryo research has the potential to contribute to fundamental research on fertility and infertility and hence to the prevention and treatment of disease. This accords with the Christian belief in a healing, redeeming God, opening the way to human participation in

---

4. Jones, "An Exploration of Religiously-Based Opposition to Clinical and Scientific Interference with the Embryo."

God's work in relieving suffering, bringing healing, and establishing justice. Examples such as these could be readily understood by committee members since they pointed towards potential benefits of the research and the significance of the quality of the scientific questions being addressed. In light of this, a number of organizations saw a place for supporting those in need of healing as long as the benefits outweighed the harms and if the use of stem cells or other approaches can be justified clinically. By directing attention away from sole reliance upon the protection of embryos, and by extending the debate to the wider community, committee members were able to connect with the messages being conveyed.

A helpful contribution from a protectionist stance was that of a Roman Catholic Bioethics Centre. Its fundamental premise was the inviolate dignity of the human embryo, leading to the inevitable conclusion that no form of embryo destruction could be considered morally licit. There is, it argued, to be no deviation from the stance that the human embryo has an absolute right to life from the moment of fertilization. The impression was given that the use of surplus embryos for research is ethically and theologically more problematic than allowing them to thaw.

This case study illustrates how public debate on ways of dealing with human embryos tends to be swayed by religious voices that oppose any interference with embryos. They do not of necessity reflect schools of theological thought that attempt to attain equipoise between the respective values of human embryos and those likely to benefit in future from this research. By casting the spotlight exclusively onto embryos and their status, these viewpoints ignore the clinical and scientific possibilities, and hence it is this one-dimensional message that frequently dominates the religious contribution to public debate.

It became very evident that many of the submissions from religious groups did not back up their position on embryo research with arguments. Their opposition was stated dogmatically and unequivocally, an approach that makes little headway in the public square. For me, the stances acceptable to an in-group using the terminology and concepts of their group are foreign to those external to the group. An ability to translate the language is essential if viewpoints are to be understandable to those in the public square.

Seeking Common Ground

As I have sat on committees receiving wide-ranging ethical and policy advice, my hope has been that church and other Christian organizations would provide values and directives that would enhance decision-making on embryo research. I do not have to know the details of how these values have been arrived at, but I do need to recognize their relevance for the clinical and scientific questions at stake. Generally, there is a clear distinction between views seeking to protect the well-being of all those involved in the decision-making and utilitarian approaches that are limited to quality-of-life considerations and society's interests. Thankfully, there is helpful Christian input, but sadly far too much is driven by doctrinaire pursuits that contribute little to public debate.[5]

The dominance of what amounts to an anti-science, or irrelevance-of-science, standpoint poses problems for the influence that religious voices can have on public debate other than to serve as voices that repeatedly oppose latest developments. This perpetual negativity does religious perspectives a disservice and fails society as much as it does the religious communities themselves. Some theologians actually reject a "common morality" approach, limiting the potential for theologians to contribute to discussion of contemporary bioethical problems.[6] As an antidote, consider the following suggestions.

In the first place, we should seek common ground and common values rather than adopt impregnable and inflexible positions, especially when dealing with novel procedures in a state of ethical and clinical flux. A problem with certain religious positions is that they assume that their insights into questions such as the moral status of the *in vitro* embryo are infallible and are the only legitimate interpretation of the scriptural record. Consequently, their insights have to be accepted by everyone else, including those who do not accept the validity of their theologically-derived premises. By the same token, some secular thinkers claim the opposite, that the *in vitro* embryo lacks any moral standing. From their diametrically different positions, both agree on one thing—they reject the notion that any common ground exists and hence accept that productive dialogue is impossible.

---

5. Examples are provided by Peterson, *Genetic Turning Points: The Ethics of Human Genetic Intervention*, and Peterson, *Changing Human Nature: Ecology, Ethics, Genes, and God*.

6. See discussion in Messer, *Respecting Life: Theology and Bioethics*, 54–76. Note his discussion of public engagement, including his overview of the stances of theologians Michael Banner, Karl Barth, Robin Gill, Celia Deane-Drummond, and Stanley Hauerwas.

Decision-making bodies have to be helped to find a way through this apparent impasse.

In the second place, all sides have to make explicit their core values and whether there actually is some overlap between the positions. Do they have any goals in common, no matter how different they appear on the surface? There has to be recognition that we live in pluralist cultures and that most people are seeking scientific advances to what seem to be intractable medical problems. One way forward may involve embryo research, the genetic editing of embryos, and even germ line gene therapy. This is not inevitable, and each proposal has to be closely monitored and rigorously assessed. Alongside this has to be placed the development of vaccines, a well-established transformative measure in controlling infectious diseases, so prominent during the COVID-19 pandemic. The connection between the use of aborted fetal tissue and the development of vaccines has shone light onto the need to balance esoteric ethical qualms and the immediate pressure to save countless lives (chapter 4).

My unfashionable view of the 1984 Warnock Report in the United Kingdom was that it achieved a tentative, if controversial, balance between opposing values.[7] At the time it was roundly condemned by many protagonists, including by Christian thinkers. Its limitation of embryo research to fourteen days gestation has stood the test of time (well over thirty-five years), even though there are voices now being raised against this limit. There was nothing definitive about this delineation, but it seemed to identify enough commonalities, both moral and scientific, to convince policymakers of its virtues. My positivity towards the Warnock Report will be seen as heresy by many fellow Christians, who have railed against its liberalism since it first appeared. It is true there are many aspects of the Report that can be critiqued, and there can be no doubt it has laid the foundation for very liberal legislation in the United Kingdom. However, nothing that has followed from it was inevitable, and it sought to find consensus and a way forward in highly contested territory. This is typical of the public sphere regardless of one's own ethical inclinations.

Third, there are no watertight answers to fiendishly new developments, and we all should be grateful for the various perspectives brought to the debate even when these stem from premises foreign to our own. Religious perspectives, including my own, generally bring to the debate a cautionary

---

7. Warnock, *Report of the Committee of Inquiry into Human Fertilisation and Embryology*.

perspective that may have implications for the source of embryos to be used in research. This will satisfy neither end of the pro- and anti-research spectrum, but it provides fertile ground for dialogue and constructive assessment within the boundary of moderately liberal legislation. There is a substantial gulf between this approach and a doggedly protectionist one, but there is an equally large gulf between it and an ideologically utilitarian one. It represents a middle ground that for me has much to commend it.

Those with religious voices need to reflect together on the core thrusts of their varying positions and how these can best serve society at large. Openness to dialogue is central if religious perspectives are to be integrated into the diverse concerns and interests of those in a pluralist society. But this will only occur when those with religious perspectives regard themselves as integral to society and capable of making a contribution that will stand alongside, and complement, a range of other perspectives. Ongoing negativity will ensure their isolation within the debating chambers of society.

Christians, both individually and in community, need to reflect on what they wish to be known for. Is it for their rejection of new developments within society, or is it their standing for the gospel? Do they want to be known for their "no" responses to many social and technological changes, or for their upright character and their adherence to the central truths of the gospel of Jesus Christ? This does not mean they are to mindlessly accept every change around them, nor that they are to refrain from arguing against developments that appear to contravene fundamental Christian stances. But they are to pick their fights and argue their cases from a Christian base. The last thing Christians should be known for is their ready acceptance of conservative social values (or, for other Christians, their acceptance of the latest liberal trends) regardless of whether or not these are based on fundamental Christian truths. Every stance should strive to be biblically informed within a context provided by a serious reading of other input, including relevant scientific input.

Advocating for Embryo Research—An Uneasy Position

It will have become eminently clear that I have dual starting points, that of a biomedical scientist and that of a Christian who looks to Scripture for theological guidance. These starting points are complementary and together provide a balanced appreciation of the potential scientific and clinical benefits but with an equally rich appreciation of scientific and human limitations. I am crucially aware of the importance of informed ethical decision-making, and that poor judgment and unrealistic expectations may cloud the moral ecosystem. I am also aware that these technologies may intrude dangerously into the sanctum of prenatal life.

These considerations lead to a number of questions. What is the scientific and clinical justification for any procedure that will destroy and/or manipulate embryos? What does the procedure tell us about our view of the value and status of these embryos? Are we exploiting them as if they are merely goods to be traded and disposed of, or are they being employed with serious intent likely to usher in beneficial prospects for mankind? How far do the biblical data at our disposal take us, and is there a point beyond which biblical data do not take us? Where does God as creator and redeemer fit into the endeavor? We simply cannot ignore questions along these lines, but as we do they take us into more probing queries about embryos.

The first is that we should not fall into the trap of physicalism. This has been a criticism within Roman Catholic circles of Vatican teaching on the embryo.[8] The thrust of this criticism is that to base one's moral teaching regarding reproductive and sexual ethics exclusively on the early embryo as a physical entity is to ignore the significance of the personal and social aspects of our lives. This is not to demean embryos, but it is an attempt to broaden the ethical discussion to take account of how we use embryos and, if we undertake embryo research, how we utilize the results of that research. Embryos are part of the human community, not some isolated sub-community—whether privileged or neglected. The ethical argument then moves from the status of the embryo to the wellbeing of the impoverished and hungry and to ask what modern medicine and medical research can achieve to alleviate appalling health inequalities and suffering. These considerations do not prejudge what may or may not be done with and for embryos, but they force us to extend our vistas beyond one isolated issue that is well-nigh incapable of resolution and consensus.

Closely related to this is a second criticism, namely, that using the status of the embryo as the starting point for the whole of reproductive ethics is to look to the past rather than to the future. This emphasizes the importance of derivation rather than benefit, allied with which is emphasis upon non-maleficence, how to avoid doing harm to the early embryo, rather than beneficence, doing good for others. Theologically, it has been

---

8. Deane-Drummond, "Bodies in Glass: A Virtue Approach to Ethical Quandaries in a Cyborg Age Through a Recovery of Practical Wisdom," 61–79.

argued that our human essence is found in our destiny rather than in our origin, and that the promise of redemption assures us that our future is not restrictively determined by our past.[9]

Third, a further implication of this stance is unwillingness to lay too much store by genetic uniqueness and genetic determinism. This demonstrates excessive dependence upon the ethical and theological significance of the inbuilt genetic characteristics of the newly fertilized zygote. If due note is not taken of the many environmental influences that make us what we will become, we will be seen as little more than the products of impersonal forces external to ourselves. This exhibits a form of classical determinism that sits very uneasily alongside the importance of our response to the overtures of God, and that we be conformed to the likeness of Christ.

In deciding what can or cannot be done to and with embryos, it is the nature of the decision-making that is crucial. The options are broadening all the time as early embryos (blastocysts) can be produced in an increasing number of ways. The choices are serious ones, between blastocysts capable of developing further and those incapable of doing so, between blastocysts that will likely develop into healthy individuals and those that will not. And do blastocysts derived from adult tissue deserve the same degree of protection as those from sperm and eggs? And if so, why? A basic principle may well be that the use of blastocysts in research should be governed by a serious therapeutic rationale and the well-grounded hope that it will lead to an improvement in the welfare of individuals and the community, regardless of their origin. In my view it is here that we should be directing serious theological reflection rather than at whether blastocysts should ever be used at all.

An additional criterion may be that any use of human embryos should be a last resort, only to be employed when there are no viable alternatives. And then there is the legitimacy or otherwise of the science itself. Are we, as societies, becoming too dependent upon technological inroads into reproduction? Are we becoming obsessed with biological normality? Questions of this nature do not presuppose particular answers but serve to make us cautious of technological imperialism.

It is also important that we make explicit the implications of what it is we are doing. If human embryos are destroyed, either clinically or in research, there is an underlying assumption that these particular embryos do not image God. But what does that mean? Are we able to say? These

---

9. Peters, *Playing God: Science, Theology and Ethics.*

are theological questions that arise in these experimental situations and yet this is far from a novel situation, since numerous human embryos are lost in all forms of reproduction, very often due to chromosomal abnormalities. And in practice it is the embryos that go on to become babies that we most revere, and not the extremely early embryos that (unknowingly) succumb. In IVF, most of the surplus embryos no longer required for reproductive purposes are eventually destroyed, suggesting that they are valued less highly than those that are now children. While it may be claimed that the latter image God, what about those that end up surplus to requirements?

For many, questions of this nature are outlandish, since they point in directions humans should never even contemplate. This is where serious ethical and theological reflection enters the picture. We are treading on holy ground, where the utmost seriousness is demanded of all of us, no matter where our thinking takes us. There is a great deal we do not know. And so, it is useful to bear in mind the words of the preacher in Ecclesiastes 11:5: "Just as you do not know how the breath comes to the bones in the mother's womb, so you do not know the work of God, who makes everything." We live in the midst of uncertainties, and on so many occasions our insights into the work of God are deficient. Balancing the welfare and aspirations of competing groups is far from easy, requiring discernment, wisdom, and a willingness to go on learning in an ever-changing world. The perplexity of our beginnings is set to increase rather than decrease. Unfortunately, our judgment constantly turns out to be flawed; we are let down and we let others down.

What is important is *what kind of people* we are. What is our moral commitment to others, including all those who are not quite like us, and how do we learn to recognize the human face in others? This will not provide neat ethical answers, but it does frame the ethical debate and the hard thinking involved in this.

8

Gender Issues

Same-Sex Attraction

Entering Divisive Territory

I ENTERED THIS TERRITORY with considerable hesitation. My repeated experience of conflict within Christian circles ensured that I did not wish to add yet another conflict topic to my already impressive conflict CV. However, the members of a discussion group that I lead at my church were like the persistent widow in Luke 18; they repeatedly requested in-depth discussion of this topic, and in the end I relented. The context for the people in this group is that of a church with a traditional stance that unfortunately is not prepared to discuss this topic openly. Assumptions are made, and it is known by many within the congregation that there is no room for same-sex-attracted people in any leadership role within the church. This assumption could be wrong, but the fact that no open discussion of it occurs means that others have to draw their own conclusions. Some within the church are unhappy with this state of affairs; hence the strong pressure on me to provide a forum for safe debate in the group I run.

The originally scheduled single meeting was quickly seen to be inadequate, and it morphed into a series of four meetings, two of which were devoted to putting forward the positions of those conservative Christians with a traditional position and then to those with a revisionist position. In each case I used the words of writers representing the respective viewpoints. I wanted them to speak for themselves, and I wanted to respect them equally and fairly. Subsequent to that series of meetings, I have had many requests for the handouts I had provided.

Research into homosexuality raises significant questions about what is "normal." Any attempt to answer this question will be determined by the standards held and the framework employed, whether biological, social, or theological. Consequently, a definitive answer that all could accept is probably unachievable. What is more, the picture is further complicated by whether sexual orientation is viewed as a dichotomy or a continuum. If it is a dichotomy, one could theoretically classify one as normal and the other as abnormal. But if it is a continuum, individuals are a mixture of normality and abnormality, a distinction so blurred as to be unhelpful. In addition, the terms "normal" and "abnormal" are pejorative and incite fear and prejudice, making analysis of homosexuality a very murky exercise. Unfortunately, so much of the debate from all angles uses the simplistic homosexual/heterosexual distinction, a distinction that is fraught with limitations.

Definitions and Scientific Evidence

At the heart of the debate is the question of whether homosexuality is a disorder, and yet it is not often tackled head-on. The reason may be that the answer will have major consequences for the way in which those who are not same-sex attracted relate to those who are attracted to members of the same sex. If it is a disorder, it follows that others should do what they can to cure it, in the same manner in which we do our best to treat the results of a genetic aberration, as outlined in chapter 5 on cystic fibrosis. We accept that the individual is suffering from a disease, and our aim is to assist them in whatever way we can. And so, if homosexuality is a disease, what follows? The logical consequence appears to be to treat their sexual identity using some form of conversion or reparative therapy, to change their homosexual attractions into heterosexual ones. This is the world of the ex-gays, where ex-gays have over the years run many of the treatment centers aimed at changing an individual's sexual orientation. The aim is to rid the individual of the "false image" they have of themselves. It is to turn one sexual instinct into another. Over the years the treatment has taken different forms; it may involve receiving electric shocks while watching gay porn, dictating how one dresses, and being given the message that being gay is equivalent to being led astray by Satan. Reparative therapy has come in for severe criticism, including by ex-leaders of the movement, as well as in society at large, to the extent that it is now banned in a number of countries. The underlying ethos of the conversion therapy approach is that being same-sex-attracted is problematic and being gay is a form of brokenness in need of God's healing.

But if reparative therapy is inappropriate, what does this tell us about the notion that homosexuality is a disease? Perhaps the only conclusion to be drawn is that it is not a disease in the usual sense, regardless of one's views on its ethical or theological legitimacy. What then is it? Is it simply an alternative to the far more usual heterosexuality? If it is an alternative, is it an acceptable alternative for Christians who aim to live their lives from a biblical base? Or is it totally unacceptable since it is mired in sin? Phrasing the dilemma in these terms demonstrates that for Christians there is an uneasy mix of different forms of evidence—scientific, psychological, cultural, and theological. It also shows that in some church circles theological considerations dominate to the exclusion of other inputs.

It is possible to analyze same-sex attraction at a purely scientific level and as a purely scientific phenomenon.[1] While this will not cover all the issues that need to be assessed, to ignore this approach is to bypass a crucial piece of evidence in understanding those who are same-sex-attracted. In scientific terms, sexual attraction refers to erotic desire experienced towards other individuals. This exists along a continuum, from attraction exclusively towards the opposite sex (OSA) to attraction exclusively towards the same sex (SSA). In the middle there is attraction to both sexes equally. The Kinsey scale that is used to measure sexual attraction ranges from 0 (exclusively OSA) to 6 (exclusively SSA). In practice this scale is collapsed to reflect the continuum of sexual attraction: OSA (0–1), bisexual (2–4), and SSA (5–6).

Uncertainty and Bias

The problem here is that measuring same-sex attraction is notoriously difficult. For instance, a person who experiences same-sex attraction may not engage in same-sex behavior, and someone who identifies as straight may experience some degree of SSA. Overall, it appears that 80–90 percent of individuals have a stable sexual attraction or sexual self-identity across their lifespan. Only a minority experience lability in sexual attraction over time.

---

1. Whiteway and Alexander, "Understanding the Causes of Same-Sex Attraction," 17–40.

The majority of SSA individuals develop stable same-sex attractions in early puberty, with a median age of ten for men and twelve for women. The prevalence of a degree of same-sex attraction across an individual's lifespan is 6–8 percent for men and 9–10 percent for women; exclusive same-sex attraction is 2 percent for men and <1 percent for women. Any same-sex behavior across the lifespan is 5 percent for men and 2 percent for women; exclusive same-sex behavior is 1 percent for men and <1 percent for women. Figures such as these should be treated with caution and not interpreted too dogmatically.

In considering these figures, distinctions have to be made between sexual orientation, sexual identity, and sexual behavior. Sexual orientation is the direction of enduring sexual-romantic desire and attraction and is largely biological in origin. Sexual identity, on the other hand, refers to an individual's self-understanding and the labelling adopted by an individual and appears to be socially influenced. Sexual behavior refers to choices and patterns in sexual activity. Culture seems to have a role in creating a context either for rejecting or accepting those with different sexual orientations. However, as psychologist David Myers, a Christian, concludes: "Yet whether a culture condemns or accepts homosexuality, heterosexuality prevails and homosexuality survives."[2]

Evidence is sparse for a role of personal choice in determining one's attraction to those of the same or the opposite sex, but it appears to be a causal factor in only a very small number of SSA individuals. This is not surprising if homosexuals generally realize they are SSA by the age of around twelve years.

Why does homosexuality exist? Common explanations range from social constructionism ("my parents made me do it") to biological essentialism ("my genes made me do it"). The argument goes something like this: "I cannot avoid being what I am—I was made like this. I have no option." An explanation like this should leave us worried; it is reminiscent of the violent person's or the alcoholic's plea that they are prisoners to their bodies and inclinations. They are claiming they cannot be held responsible for how they act. Are all of us nothing more than prisoners of our bodies and constitutions, our brains and our genes? Or is this misleading?

Enormous care is required at this point. The scientific inquiry into highly contested realms like homosexuality may be far from neutral. There are substantial political and moral considerations at stake, and these may

2. Myers, *Psychology*, 428.

have had some bearing on scientific research, particularly in terms of the manner in which it is reported. One of the difficulties is that research tends to be conducted using a dichotomous definition of heterosexuality and homosexuality: it is one or the other. But this oversimplifies the situation. And then there is the problem posed by the limitations imposed upon quantitative research, since it is nearly always exceedingly difficult to get a representative sample to participate in the research, let alone a large enough sample to make the study statistically significant. Sample sizes are frequently limited due to the low frequency of homosexuality in the general population, while even recruiting subjects is fraught with complications, since prevalent homophobia may limit the number of those who are prepared to participate.

Investigations into environmental causes include the respective contributions of parenting and phobia, childhood abuse, and the experience of trauma, and socialization. Biological causes, in turn, span genetics—twin studies, the possible role of specific genes, the fraternal birth order effect, sex and gender atypicality, and associated neurological features. After assessing this range of possible contributory factors, Whiteway and Alexander made the following observations.[3]

- No one causal model has gained sufficient support to provide a compelling explanation by itself.
- There is no "gay gene."
- While there is support for the fraternal birth order effect, there is no firm evidence for an immunological explanation for this observation.
- In women, exposure to elevated androgen levels can lead to developmental changes causing an attraction to women.
- There is no positive evidence that SSA is due to the effects of socialization, personal choice, poor parenting, or having a brain of the "wrong sex."
- Sexual attraction is a highly complex trait, so that different influences may be more important at different times and in different cultures.
- Not all homosexual men carry the same variant genes, and not all homosexual women are masculinized.

---

3. Whiteway and Alexander, "Understanding the Causes of Same-Sex Attraction," 40.

They concluded: "The social and cultural environment in which people live is constantly changing, including their friends and partners, together with their own motivations and aspirations, creating a complex system in which biological make-up is integrated with multiple environmental, social, and cultural factors. Consequently, there is no single definitive cause of same-sex attraction."[4] Hence the frequently encountered multifactorial models highlighting the intermingling of genetic and environmental factors to produce SSA inclinations and behavior. A number of stimuli or substrates may push an individual in one direction or another, but this is not equivalent to being forced to act in predetermined ways. Ultimately, though, individuals are morally responsible for their behavior, and homosexuality should not be dismissed simply as a "sin."

An often-cited analogy for homosexuality is alcoholism, which, though limited, provides a valuable illustration. The influence of genetics in predisposing a person to alcoholism is well supported, although it is not the only factor—the environment has considerable influence. If a similar causation lies behind homosexuality, a similar morality must be applied. Most people do not blame the alcoholic for having a tendency towards alcoholism, only for failing to restrain the urge to overindulge in alcohol. Perhaps a similar approach should be adopted towards the person with homosexual desires, censuring them only for expressing them in homosexual acts if that is one's moral and theological stance. By the same token, a similar approach should be taken towards OSA individuals, with their heterosexual desires and sexual behavior.

Regardless of what moral stance one takes, it is becoming clear that telling those who are same-sex-attracted to refrain from indulging in homosexual acts, that is, in any sexual activity, equates with telling them to be celibate. It is not surprising that those SSA Christians who are determined to be celibate may face unending struggle even as they consider that this is the Lord's way for them. There is no exact parallel for heterosexuals, even for single OSA women, who long for a child because they feel unfulfilled without one, let alone without a partner. There are, of course, similarities and comparable spiritual battles, but they do not face quite the finality and opprobrium of SSA individuals. In many churches single women are regarded as integral to the church community and readily accepted even if outside traditional family structures. Single gay men or lesbian women do not fit as readily into this environment, even when cautiously welcomed.

4. Whiteway and Alexander, "Understanding the Causes of Same-Sex Attraction," 40.

Although the scientific basis of same-sex attraction is far from definitive, it is unhelpful to ignore it altogether or even bypass it in theological assessments of the phenomenon. It should also have a part to play in pastoral responses to all who are same-sex attracted. Once again, the science-faith duopoly comes into view, underlining the role these scientific insights have to play in a holistic response to what many within Christian circles regard as a perplexing situation.

Christian Traditionalists and Revisionists

Debate within the church revolves around five biblical passages or incidents: Sodom and Gomorrah (Gen 19; Judg 19; Jude 7), largely abandoned today; Leviticus 18:22; 20:13; Romans 1:26–27; 1 Corinthians 6:9; and 1 Timothy 1:10. I have never seen it as my role to pontificate on the appropriate interpretation of these passages, since I am neither a biblical scholar nor a theologian. In saying this I find myself in the company of the preponderance of Christians, and to me it is invidious to take sides on matters beyond my expertise. Inevitably, I end up being more attracted by one set of interpretations than another, but this is an amalgam of arguments and analyses aimed at being as true to an authentic Christian position as I can attain—nothing more and nothing less. I claim no infallibility of any description.

Traditionalists adopt a interpretation of the biblical passages normally seen as condemning homosexual behavior and reject the recent intellectual, social, and political changes advancing a "gay agenda." The latter is seen as going against the biblical mandate for human sexuality. The homosexual issue is regarded as a sexual-sin or sexual-perversity issue. Traditionalists either do not accept the concept of sexual orientation, or they reject any legitimacy for same-sex orientation. They see it as a further extension of sexual libertarianism and are alarmed by the advances of the gay culture in Western societies. They do not want to see any inroads of this culture into the churches or Christian organizations. In other words, they want to hold on to what they understand to be traditional Christian and/or cultural attitudes and practices, including biblical interpretations, church practices, cultural attitudes, and state/national laws. The result is rejection of practices associated with the LGBTQI (lesbian, gay, bisexual, transgender, queer, and intersexed) community.

They believe in the transformative power of God to enable LGBTQI Christians to sustain a life of celibacy; some consider that God will change a person's sexual orientation. For them the sacredness of the institution of traditional marriage between a man and a woman reigns supreme since it is based on the divine creation order in Genesis. For them any challenge to the sexual complementarity of the divine creation order is to challenge historic Christianity and the whole of the Christian tradition on sexual morality. The question for traditionalists is whether there is any place at all for LGBTQI Christians in their churches unless their sexual orientation is never divulged. If they do, will they be welcomed as fellow believers? Different traditionalists respond to this question in a variety of ways.

For instance, what some term "moderate traditionalism" seeks to offer non-judgmental acceptance of LGBTQI people but is unwilling to approve of LGBTQI sexual relationships. This position has been further subdivided into sides A and B. The more permissive side A Christians believe it is morally permissible in God's sight for gay and lesbian people to enter covenantal-marital same-sex relationships (but not promiscuous ones). The more restrictive side B Christians do not consider this as morally permissible, although they consider that LGBTQI people should be welcomed into church life. It soon becomes clear that there is a clash of perspectives here, with two conflicting loyalties—to the Christian tradition on the one hand and to LGBTQI people on the other. Both look to biblical teaching, since both seek to locate moral authority and reliability in the Scriptures. Their respective emphases, though, differ, and they both face the challenge of balancing the judgmental and pastoral sides of these equations. What they are both doing to varying extents is seek a place for LGBTQI Christians in their midst.

No matter how far the various traditionalist categories extend, it is a further jump to "revisionists," who accept to varying degrees the legitimacy within the church of those in gay relationships. They want to see change happen in biblical interpretations, church practices, cultural attitudes, and state/national laws in search of at least a more humane context for LGBTQI people to live their lives. This revisionist position goes further than the moderate traditionalist stance because for revisionists any traditional position leaves LGBTQI people as second-class citizens unable to exercise to the full their spiritual gifts in the life of the church. They find it implausible that Jesus would give them anything less than full embrace and a full place at the table.

Besides those who are prepared to be explicit about their stance, there are also the "avoiders," those who want to avoid taking sides on this issue for as long as possible until they are forced into it by circumstances. These individuals and churches want to evade the subject for a variety of reasons, including genuine convictional uncertainty, fear of hurting people, and fear of conflict and schism.

Traditionalists include SSA individuals who are celibate and live alone (some of these are ministers in churches) and SSA individuals who are married and live in a family with children. The more permissive moderate traditionalists include SSA individuals who are celibate but living with homosexual partners. Revisionists include SSA individuals living with homosexual partners, and who may be celibate or in active sexual partnerships.

None of these distinctions is without problems and uncertainties. They tend to be theoretical and are to some extent arbitrary. Furthermore, labels are always dangerous. But what they are trying to do is highlight points of demarcation and bring into the open the beliefs and attitudes that allow a Christian community to be open, or not, to SSA individuals. They are clearing the ground and hopefully are opening the door to more enlightened dialogue.

Encountering Homosexuality: Meeting SSA Individuals Face-to-Face

The major contribution made by theological ethicist David Gushee[5] and pastor Ken Wilson[6] is the way in which these "straight" pastors have changed their views on the place of SSA individuals in the church as a result of interacting with them as fellow believers. This is not an inevitable consequence of dealing with SSA Christians, since there are vicars in the Anglican Church, for instance, who are SSA but who are celibate and have a traditional position on homosexuality. Nevertheless, coming face-to-face with fellow believers brings the debate into focus as it brings with it profound pastoral dimensions. An additional perspective is provided by those with family members who are SSA, whether siblings or children, when the human face of same-sex attraction becomes very personal.

David Gushee put it very succinctly when he stated that his mind and heart had been changed as God sent large numbers of "sexual others" into his life. For him, these experiences gradually led to a sharpening of his understanding of the Christian gospel and the Christian church and to fresh thinking about what Christian sexual ethics should look like. In

5. Gushee, *Changing Our Mind*.
6. Wilson, *A Letter to My Congregation*.

light of this, he felt obligated before God and these new Christian friends to let others know about this change and encourage others to follow him. From his perspective what had changed was not his view of the Bible but of traditionalist readings of certain texts in the Bible. In turn, other texts about the gospel message and the church took on new meaning to include the full embrace of gays and lesbians.

His concern is now with the church's attitudes towards LGBTQI people and the degree to which Christians in the church are willing to welcome them as fellow members of the body of Christ. For him, this entails revisiting questions of exegesis and sexual ethics, and this led him to a revisionist position. The result is that he has been dismissed by many Evangelicals in the United States while the more extreme question his status as a Christian. This illustrates the harshness of some of the debate and the tragic disunity within some more conservative strands of the church. This, in part, is because Gushee sides with LGBTQI Christians, whom he regards as a despised minority within the church. The one central stricture from him is that homosexual relationships have to be ones of covenant faithfulness, a faithfulness not always found, as he reminds his readers, within heterosexual relationships.

Ken Wilson's perspective commences from his rejection of the binary choice between the two dominant stances on homosexuality: what he calls the "love the sinner, hate the sin" and the "open and affirming" positions. For him these equate with the conservative-liberal divide between those who are seen as being faithful to God versus those who are unfaithful to God, depending of course on one's viewpoint. This approach involves moral judgment that divides congregations. In light of his pastoral experiences, he recognized a third way, a path that emphasizes acceptance over either affirmation or exclusion. He noted that the exclusionary approach does great harm to SSA individuals, keeping them away from church and from Christian community. The gay Christians he encountered did not seem like hardened sinners, such as those condemned in Scripture and frequently associated with the derogatory "homosexual lifestyle." He writes that he returned time and again to his duty as a pastor. "As a pastor, I have responsibility to Jesus to care for his sheep to the best of my ability. I simply couldn't shake the growing conviction that enforcing the traditional exclusion of gay people seemed inconsistent with that duty."[7]

---

7. Wilson, *A Letter to My Congregation*, loc. 832.

Gender Issues

For Wilson this became a very serious issue when seen alongside the church's accommodations for the divorced and remarried, practices largely condemned in Scripture and yet tolerated by churches, while enforcing exclusionary policies against gay people. For him, any actions that cause an unnecessary disincentive to follow Christ are as serious as failing to uphold a moral good. After a careful reading of the passages central to the homosexual debate, he concluded that temple prostitution, pederasty, and slave sex are worlds removed from the couples in his church with same-sex attraction from childhood and living in faithful covenantal relationships. He failed to see how these couples could be accused of having been given over to shameful lusts as punishment for gross and persistent idolatry. For him the context, tone, and application of the biblical passages did not fit the people he was thinking about.

Wilson speaks of what he terms "pre-exclusion" in churches, whereby certain categories of people know they will not feel welcome in a given church. Examples he gives are scientists in evangelical congregations who do not feel welcome because the churches oppose evolution and, of course, gays on the grounds that they will be rejected. Wilson writes: "Stigmatizing a vulnerable minority is something we should repent of, not something we should perpetuate."[8] In light of this, he came to the conclusion that SSA is a *disputable matter*, and he found the way forward in Romans 14–15, where Paul seeks to cope with two groups in the church, the "weak" and the "strong." The former were vegetarians and observed special days; the latter ate meat and largely did not observe special days. Scholars have been prepared to equate the weak with modern-day conservatives bound by the strictures of the law and the strong as closer to liberals and relatively free of these strictures. While one should not push these parallels too far, Paul's concern appears to have been that the existence of these two distinct groups threatened the unity of the church in Rome. Under no circumstances should they be allowed to divide one group of believers from another, since this would jeopardize the well-being of the gospel.

Wilson's answer lies in a third approach, that of "acceptance." The core of this approach is to be willing to disagree amicably with each other within the church even though you disagree on this particular disputable question. The different groups do not separate from each other but continue to hold their respective positions as firmly as their consciences dictate. They accept that they do not have to agree on this question in order to be one in the

---

8. Wilson, *A Letter to My Congregation*, loc. 1376.

Spirit. Wilson's third way asks people who differ on this question to accept each other as Christ has accepted them without predicating acceptance on affirming the other's lifestyle in this and many other moral questions. In his church this is practiced on numerous matters, including remarriage, how much consumption amounts to greed, and the use of IVF as a reproductive technology. They embrace these demands because they believe this way of relating to each other bears a formidable witness to the power of the gospel. Acceptance of each other recognizes that individually we each stand or fall as unto the Lord.

For Wilson, Romans 14 urges the church to err on the side of inclusion when confronted by a disputable matter, thereby practicing acceptance and embrace as against exclusion. This approach does not abrogate discussion or disagreement but encourages all to respect each other as people of integrity and as people whose ultimate responsibility is to Christ. All are to accept one another as Christ has accepted them. The continued co-existence of strongly held convictions demonstrates the power of the gospel to create a firm foundation of unity.

Encountering Homosexuality: Maintaining Traditional Boundaries

Both Gushee and Wilson have moved away from traditionalism, and both are open to accepting evangelical gay Christians and Christian couples. Both want to retain a biblical base, and both take biblical teaching seriously. Andrew Goddard represents a traditionalist within Anglicanism, but one who is well aware of the competing forces at play.[9] For him the overall tenor of the biblical teaching about sexuality leads him to reject homosexual conduct, so much so that this would apply even apart from the specific biblical texts on the subject. No matter how important mutual love and covenantal faithfulness may be, he argues that they are never commended as sufficient to justify a sexual relationship outside of marriage. He acknowledges that Jesus never mentioned homosexuality, but contends that in his day the law was understood to prohibit all homosexual conduct. In short, homosexual conduct is one sign of humanity's rejection of God's creation purpose.

Goddard's approach is enlightening, since he is prepared to accept that all our understanding is provisional and so we must be humble when we disagree with those of a different persuasion. He also states that we may

9. Goddard, *Homosexuality and the Church of England*.

have to revise our reading of Scripture in light of new understanding and fresh insights into the text. In line with this, he accepts that the church has changed its mind over a variety of issues, including divorce and remarriage and the role of women in the church (although many traditionalists would not agree with this stance). He also accepts that traditionalists have to listen to the biographical testimonies of gay Christians, and that the church should face up to the challenge of restating traditional teaching in terms of today's culture with its essentialist conceptions of sexual orientation. Goddard claims that while gay people should be supported, and the good in gay relationships should be acknowledged, major problems for the church would ensue were it to authorize such unions.

In view of Wilson's proposals, it is interesting to hear Goddard contending that ways have to be found of entering into dialogue with non-traditionalists, warmly welcoming them but still upholding a traditional Christian understanding of sexuality. This is encouraging, but there is no indication as to how this can be achieved and how the church can be seen as a welcoming community rather than one that is, at best, ambivalent towards gay people and at worst dangerous for them. What is surprising is that Goddard accepts remarriage after divorce and yet still maintains that any sexual relationships outside marriage (which in strict biblical terms is for life) are against the ethos of Scripture. On these grounds same-sex unions are dismissed as contrary to Scripture.

There appears to be a contradiction here, and a different set of expectations depending upon whether one is heterosexual or homosexual. This inconsistency allows a church to be conservative on homosexuality but far less so on heterosexuality. I find this lack of consistency difficult to comprehend, and one can hardly be surprised if LGBTQI Christians feel they are not made welcome. One wonders what this says about our unity in the body of Christ. These comments have nothing to do with the interpretation of the core biblical passages but about how we treat one another as fellow Christians and how we determine who are fellow Christians.

In view of these considerations, I end up with considerable sympathy with Wilson's emphasis upon acceptance rather than affirmation and exclusion. This makes no attempt to legislate definitively on the rightness or wrongness of either of the major positions, but one has to ask whether we should be attempting this. For me, as for Wilson, Romans 14 (particularly verses 1–4, 19, 20) is transformative.

Nevertheless, there is a proviso. These verses will only be seen as crucial if one agrees that issues surrounding same-sex Christians can rightly be regarded as disputable. If a different conclusion is reached, namely, that all SSA inclinations are deeply and irrevocably sinful, then the Christian profession of SSA individuals and couples will be rejected and their exclusion from the Christian community will follow. This is the stark contrast sometimes, but not always, encountered, although I think it is an inevitable outcome of a refusal to accept at least some legitimacy for the sexual expression of same-sex attraction.

Traditionalists who are themselves same-sex attracted provide an immensely insightful perspective into the pressures of living by this position. Ed Shaw, who is the minister of a church in England, is clear that what keeps him on the traditional path is not so much individual proof texts from Scripture or even the sheer weight of the church's traditional teaching against homosexual practice.[10] Instead, it stems from those traditions and teachings within the story of what God has done in Jesus Christ. He abstains from homosexual behavior because of the power of the scriptural story. In spite of this, he admits he is instinctively sexually attracted to a certain type of man and that there is an enormous gap between what he believes intellectually and what he instinctively feels as a matter of course. For him this is self-denial, and it is a self-denial he considers is essential to keep him faithful to Jesus, even as he is unable to live life to the full sexually.

I am deeply impressed by what Shaw writes, and he writes as a vicar. His honesty and transparency bring out the very best in the Christian faith and in the traditionalist. I cannot but admire his steadfastness and his pain. But he knows that he is only kept going by the love of the church and the friends around him. He admits that without them he would be lost. And I wonder what someone like him would be like if he was in a church culture that rejected his ministry and did not allow him to be a vicar/pastor within a church or indeed in any position of leadership.

Nate Collins again writes as a gay celibate Christian with a traditional stance.[11] He is engaged in a ministry in the United States to minister the gospel to people who are same-sex attracted. Once more, he is brutally honest about how churches in the United States seem unable to cope with gay Christians in their midst. He is looking for openings for gay people to contribute to the church, and he also recognizes that those who are not

---

10. Shaw, *The Plausibility Problem*.
11. Collins, *All but Invisible*.

LGBTQI need to learn from the contributions of their gay brothers and sisters in Christ.

He asks whether conservative churches truly have their arms open to gay people by seeking to incorporate gender and sexual minorities into their spiritual communities. He comments that following Christ faithfully in the wake of the sexual revolution involves more than simply telling gay people to abstain from immoral sexual behavior. He is explicit about the hurt and misunderstanding encountered by some gay people in churches that are more interested in condemning the "gay agenda" than in empathizing with gay believers in their midst. For him "this is a double standard made more obvious when Christian communities show signs of being soft on other, more socially acceptable sins. The Bible mentions the sin of greed far more often than the sin of same-gender sexual behavior. This seems to be a sign of imbalance."[12] A challenge such as this has considerable weight coming from a traditionalist who is same-sex attracted, and who sees the conflict from a side rarely experienced by straight critics of homosexuals in the church.

All too often one hears of Christian congregations with no idea how to cope with someone different from themselves, even when that person has for years been a major leader in their midst. I find it impossible to understand how a community which has, for many years, known and respected someone can reject them when their sexuality is made public. They had previously respected and benefitted from this individual's teaching ministry, and yet they are now no longer deemed fit to hold any leadership position. There is something amiss here, and responses such as some have had to endure display little of the grace of God or the understanding displayed by Jesus.

Contending with the "Other"

We all live in a suboptimal world, and in this world we all have to learn to compromise as we come to terms with our own sin as well as the sin of others. Our awareness of falling short, and of letting down our Lord, ourselves, our spouses, our families, and those close to us can be very hard to bear. No one lives up to an ideal, whatever that ideal may be. If only it were not so. This is a profoundly spiritual matter that influences our ethical decision-making in every area of our lives.

---

12. Collins, *All but Invisible*, 22.

At the Margins

We are surrounded by what I am calling the "suboptimal": divorce, abortion, war, long-term ill-health, and diseases present from birth. From the perspective of the traditional Christian, a lifestyle based on same-sex attraction may be regarded as suboptimal, even if this designation is vigorously rejected by others. Rarely does one find consensus among Christians on ethical questions. The task in each instance is to determine what a biblically faithful approach will look like, although biblical interpretations will vary. For some, SSA behavior is not an ideal any more than divorce or extramarital affairs are ideals, but in all these instances we have to find ways of living with each other, especially with those in any of the less-than-ideal situations.

It is highly unlikely that the divisions within the Christian church over SSA will be settled in the foreseeable future. Confining one's attention to academic niceties, no matter how major they might be thought to be, can only end up in ongoing division, with an increasing number of people being hurt. But extracting ourselves from this morass entails a willingness to moderate some of our cherished shibboleths. If we refuse to be open to committed Christians who are SSA, regardless of whether we approve or disapprove of this orientation or behavior, will cement in place the stalemate so often encountered today.

For some, this represents a lowering of moral standards, even as we have accepted other practices that at one time would also have been considered questionable, even objectionable. One can think of accepting those who have remarried following divorce, those who have married non-celibate people, women in leadership positions, women who do not wear head coverings in church services. These remain major issues for some, but have disappeared into obscurity for others. More important than the details is the realization that we live in a suboptimal world where we need to know the forgiveness and love of Christ each day. We are also to welcome those who are truly repentant and those whose interpretation of Scripture may not precisely align with ours. But this still leaves core considerations.

First, the *reliability of tradition*: how reliable is Christian tradition when assessing SSA? The Jewish establishment at the time of Jesus displayed an exaggerated loyalty to their own human traditions. Tradition is human, and no matter how useful in some areas it should be subordinate to Scripture. Consequently, long-standing interpretations of the key passages central to the SSA debate have to be analyzed and reanalyzed in the light of new information and understanding. This will not of necessity overturn the traditional understanding, but it will cause it to be assessed afresh. And this is where scientific information enters the picture—not as a means of providing a definitive answer but of illuminating the context and feeding into an all-round understanding of same-sex attraction.

Second, the *authority of Scripture:* this is not being challenged, but what is up for debate is a literalistic interpretation of the core passages and whether the socio-cultural circumstances holding in Old Testament times and in the early church and those holding today influence the way in which those Scriptures are viewed. For some there can be no changes; for others changes are essential.

Third, the *emphasis on celibacy* shines through for traditionalists. SSA individuals are expected to be celibate no matter how difficult it may be for them nor how much it militates against their sexual desires. It is at this point that they come up against their natural inclinations, as graphically depicted by SSA individuals, including those who abide by a traditional ethic. In another form it emerges for those transgender individuals who are aware from a very young age of having been born into the "wrong" body and will remain so unless they undergo procedures to change their gender. SSA individuals cannot be changed as radically as this. Traditionalists tell them they have to live with it and be celibate because this is their only option if they want to remain faithful to biblical injunctions. Is this placing too much store by celibacy, unless they have been given a gift of celibacy? And where do single heterosexual females fit into this picture, as the hope of a sexual partner recedes? SSA individuals are locked in to their state.

Fourth, for Christian revisionists, the role of a *covenantal perspective* enters center stage. For traditionalists this is inadequate, since it fails to confine sexual intercourse to a male-female lifelong marriage. And yet it strengthens the notion of commitment especially where that commitment is lifelong. Once more we are back at the question of consistency and have to ask how consistent many heterosexuals are in their lifestyle. Is more expected of SSA individuals than of others?

Fifth, for some it is important to *look beyond theology* alone to the place of reason, experience, and extrabiblical data. The relationship between the biblical text and other information at our disposal, such as scientific information about SSA, is a crucial consideration. For others this is anathema and akin to heresy. However, over the centuries, Christian theologians and writers in general have gained enormous insights into the meaning of the biblical text from external sources, as seen in changes in Bible translations as well as in Christian social practices. The church is always relating to the world around it even when it hesitates to admit it. The church also benefits from some of the movements in society, as with the increasing recognition given to women over recent decades; some of these actually help the church in its understanding of biblical teaching. The current trends in the LGBTQI world may not be to the liking of some Christians, but they recognize that current monogamous homosexual unions are strikingly different from the homosexual prostitution and idolatry that confronted the early church.

Querying the Binary Divide

A binary divide characterizes much of the homosexual debate: traditionalist against revisionist. While these two labels are legitimate ones, they also end up in a cul-de-sac and in inevitable division within the church if taken as indelible opposing perspectives. For me the following pointers represent the bottom line.

1. The gospel is for all, and all are equal in God's sight. All are in need of the gospel and all who respond to the call of Christ are to be welcome, if at all possible, in the midst of the church. Openness to others in love is a prerequisite that should be taken very seriously indeed, especially as we take seriously the notion that all have fallen short of God's standards.

2. Our aim is to be faithful to Scripture and its revelation, accepting the centrality and reliability of Scripture. However, care needs to be taken in determining how Scripture is best interpreted, taking account of the cultural and scientific context within which the various writers were functioning. This input is as relevant today as at any time in the past and is central when assessing applied ethical practice from a Christian perspective.

3. We are to look closely at whether the instances of same-sex activity recorded in both the Old and New Testaments are similar to monogamous same-sex activity in the twenty-first century. I have come to the conclusion that they are probably not equivalent, although the legitimacy of any SSA behavior has to be gauged by reference to Scripture and the central significance of a covenantal relationship.

4. Those who are SSA within the Christian community and who are seeking to be faithful to Christ should be accepted as Christ has accepted

everyone else. This applies even if one is dubious about an individual's SSA orientation and even more so with SSA behavior. This is because we are living in the "not yet" times when the kingdom of God has not fully come and we are all affected by ongoing sin and corruption.

5. This leads to the more general principle that Christian communities are to be characterized by dialogue and respect for each other, even in the face of major disagreements on some (disputable) theological matters. It is crucial that we learn to cope with diverse viewpoints without jeopardizing the integrity of others or excluding them from communion with us. This applies across a broad swathe of controversial issues within the church, of which homosexuality is just one.

6. The challenge of acting in this manner is immense, since it involves choosing the relational over the adversarial. This goes against the grain of modern conservative Christianity based as it is on distinguishing itself from liberal theology and of seeking to be faithful to Scripture in the face of rampant, aggressive, secularizing trends. This is where Paul's injunctions regarding the weak and the strong are as pertinent today as they were when he made the comments to the early churches. In adjudicating on the merits of eating meat or only vegetables, and of considering some days more sacred than others, they were not to look down on those holding the alternative position but were to serve the Lord with the whole of their lives (Rom 14:1–23; 1 Cor 8:1–13; Col 2:16; 1 Tim 4:1–16).

7. Regardless of the position adopted, an emphasis on the centrality of covenantal/faithful relationships for all is crucial, regardless of sexuality, a message that applies just as strongly to heterosexuals as homosexuals within the churches.

The Relevance of Science-Faith Borderlands

No matter how far the discussion in this chapter may have seemed to deviate from the science-faith domain, that is not the case. At all points, it has been informed by my approaches to the ongoing relationship between what we are as embodied beings and human persons in relationship to God. No one is born a blank canvas; we are all informed by our genetic, environmental, and cultural settings, leading to complex interrelationships that, for

Christians, have to be governed by their understanding of how God works and transforms all of us.

One message to have emerged from previous chapters is that, no matter how important Christians regard the Bible and its teachings, it alone, in isolation of a myriad cultural, scientific, and social factors, will not provide indelible ways forward ethically and socially. This does not decrease its significance as the word of God, but it does acknowledge its role in providing foundational guidance for the lives of God's people. It also helps determine how best we are to utilize its principles and themes as we navigate our way through what is often highly complex and uncertain territory, namely, the world in which we are located.

9

Anatomy of an Academic Life

On Being Sidelined

Two episodes of the TV series *Yes Minister/Yes Prime Minister* demonstrate unequivocally the means employed of sidelining a person for a position. One deals with the appointment of a bishop of the Church of England and the other the governor of the Bank of England. In neither case does the public service want a person of integrity to occupy the position since it is thought they will challenge the *status quo*. And so means are found of questioning their rectitude by suggesting that they believe too firmly in the foundational beliefs of Christianity in the one instance and in the need to oppose corruption in the other.

This, of course, is comedy, and by definition the issues are exaggerated in order to make a point. And yet, in both instances, the comedy has profound truths hidden just beneath the surface. Integrity and straightforward honesty are challenging to many people who are much more comfortable with half-truths and with those who will turn a blind eye to incompetence and sometimes dubious dealings. They are also comfortable with those who will not question them or suggest alternative paths and innovative ways of doing things.

These episodes resonate powerfully with me for the simple reason that this has been my experience on many occasions in a variety of settings. The academic in me comes to the fore repeatedly with the desire to want clarity and challenge what seem to me to be inconsistencies. With this in mind

At the Margins

I have been intrigued by a suggestion from theologian Roger Olson[1] that what is needed in churches and equally in other institutions is the position of "joker/jester." For him, this role is that of someone appointed and given the right without penalty to question anything. In the case of a church, it may include beliefs, customs, traditions, and habits that deserve to be questioned because they may be unhelpful and detrimental to the health of the kingdom of God. They may even be untrue but have become part of the way of thinking and acting of the church and its leaders. And exactly the same applies within academia.

I have frequently felt that I have occupied such a role, although no one has appointed me to it, and some may have resented it. I have never set myself up in opposition to accepted ways of acting and believing within the circles where I have resided. But I have felt the need to analyze and assess and, on occasion, to question and suggest that some paths may not be as straightforward and self-evidently true as assumed. In acting in this way, I have brought my scientific mindset to bear on spiritual and administrative issues, an uneasy transposition of approaches, but with the potential to chart new directions.

Sidelining is a common feature throughout society, including university and church, both of which have been central to my life as a Christian academic. In the university it is a way of ensuring that good people are not promoted to senior positions if they threaten the current dominant way of functioning, challenge unspoken assumptions, or introduce alternative ideas. It has happened to me and I have seen it happening to others. Every effort is made to bypass them and thrust them to one side. In the context of the church some people are sidelined by being kept away from preaching or being able to contribute to decision-making. The reasons are generally unclear, since they are not made explicit. Probably, they are a threat to authoritarian leaders and/or those who feel they would be unable to provide explanations for decisions being contemplated, answer queries, or stand up to probing.

These thoughts are relevant to the thrust of this book, of occupying a position "at the margins." Sidelining pushes people to the margins in the hope of keeping them there, where they are unable to query what is occurring and/or can be labelled as being irrelevant. They are excluded from ongoing decision-making, and hence cannot interfere with the thinking of

---

1. Olson, "The Joker/Jester Asks 'Why Chosen'?"

the in-group. Being outcasts, they belong to another tribe; in political terms they have been relegated to the back benches.

When sidelining is taking place within the context of highly contentious issues—the status of the embryo, the reproductive technologies, gene therapy, abortion, gender perplexity, euthanasia, to mention a few central to my interests—the lack of marginal voices will reduce the range of input into the debate. It will diminish the options to those of a select few at the expense of what might be useful, if troubling, insights from others. Sidelining also means that the group is deprived of the contributions of those who could prove valuable if only they were given the opportunity to contribute. It amounts to a closing of the ranks and the restriction of perspectives to easily agreed and well-traversed paths. As I have intimated, this is not a phenomenon restricted to churches and Christian groups, but it is more commonly encountered in groups that exist to defend what they regard as important central truths or well-established policies and practices.

Being an academic and a Christian in no way opens the door to marginalization; this is far from inevitable. But I would suggest that an inquisitive mind and a longing to be satisfied with explanations partly opens the door to a place on the outside.

Reaffirming a Basic Duality

Starting out on an academic career in 1965 in an anatomy department, I could never have envisaged that it would take me along a host of apparently circuitous paths. On the surface it looks as though not much has happened. I have remained linked to an anatomy department, although I deviated from neuroscience as my prime focus and bioethics became integral to my academic endeavors. I was also instrumental in initiating a wide range of administrative undertakings, but throughout I have sought to be guided by my Christian faith. I have never left behind my allegiance to science and the scientific method, nor to the belief that this is an important means by which God blesses humans when used wisely and with discernment. For me the broad framework within which I have functioned has been that of a robust and well-grounded Christian faith.

My digressions into bioethics have never deviated from this fundamental stance. I have remained a scientist (more specifically, anatomist) with a serious interest in applied ethics. It was this that led me into the emerging field of anatomy and ethics. At heart I am a scientist committed to the rigors of scientific analysis. The same applies to my thinking as a Christian. I have never sought to leave my science behind, an attitude that helps explain my unease whenever I encounter theologians who seek to address questions around early human development, or a viral pandemic, with practically no reference to any scientific input. For me this amounts to a denial of the whole scientific enterprise and of all the good things that God has bestowed upon his creation through the human creativity underlying science and, in my case, biomedical science. Only in this way do we get a full-orbed glimpse into God's wonderful world.

Throughout, I have sought to stress two prevailing drivers in my life: my faith and my vocation, or, more specifically, my faith as a theologically conservative Christian and my training as a biomedical scientist. I find it impossible to separate the two, since each influences and informs the other. I have often had occasion to reflect on how different I may have been had I been trained as a theologian rather than as a scientist or alternatively as a scientist with a secular worldview. While I cannot vouch for the accuracy of any predictions, I think there is little doubt that, on both counts, I would have approached applied ethical questions quite differently. I have never wanted to divide my life into distinct spiritual and secular compartments but have stressed that Christ is as relevant for my thinking about scientific and ethical matters as about church-related matters. On most occasions this is not made explicit, but the values I espouse and the hopes I cling on to are, I trust, ones emanating from the Jesus Christ as revealed in Scripture. It also means that I am committed to the view that science can, in some instances, help us come to grips with biblical interpretation.

I want people to think and be challenged so that they can work through their own responses to challenging problems. I have never viewed it as my role to provide them with ready-made answers, or with dogmatic stances in murky ethical waters. For those who are not Christians, my aim is to sketch out paths that are reasonable and that take the evidence seriously. I want fellow believers to take the Bible seriously and to use it to inform their thinking on very difficult and complex issues. Although the Bible does not provide detailed answers in many of the areas with which I deal, it has exceedingly helpful insights for those who seek to follow Christ. While I do not expect the Bible to provide categorical answers to highly complex contemporary issues, I have no doubt it contains within its pages helpful ways forward that will provide a context for responsible decision-making.

Science provides authentic glimpses into reality, and it is these that lead me to rejoice in what science has to offer. Of course, science is the work of human beings, who can be misled and can utilize it for improper purposes. It is never an unalloyed blessing. At its best, it is a means of revealing the amazing works of God and secrets of God's world. At its worst, it becomes the cornerstone of an alternative worldview, one centred on science rather than on God. The latter has nothing in common with my approach which is to see science and Scripture as two aspects of the same truth, with each contributing essential elements needed for a holistic view of God's world.

As pointed out in chapter 1, I have been unable to get away from two passages in Scripture, namely, Luke 18:17 and 1 Cor 13:12. According to the Luke passage, "whoever does not receive the kingdom of God as a little child will never enter it." In the Corinthian passage, Paul is forthright: "For now we see only a reflection, as in a mirror, but then we will see face-to-face. Now I know only in part; then I will know fully, even as I have been fully known." Both passages are counterintuitive. Who wants to act like a little child, and who wants to accept that all they have striven for is inadequate? Even more stridently, who wants to accept that each of these is an ideal that one should strive to attain? And yet this combination appears to be the Christian way, bringing together openness, honesty, and truthfulness, with a realization that our present understanding, comprehension and expertise are far from complete.

Both science and faith flourish when guided by such prerequisites, with their longing to uncover new truths, and new ways of understanding, responding as appropriate to new evidence and new insights. This may be the way of science, but is it the way of faith? A faith-based approach to reality is routinely viewed as looking to the past and the certainties of a by-gone era. This is partially correct, but it is not the whole truth, because it is primarily a response to the living God, just as science is a response to the evidence of the senses. Underlying both is the unsavory reality that our most wonderful and compelling insights are ultimately limited that will be improved upon and enhanced. The evidence for this is all around us. In the sciences the life cycle of concepts may be little more than a few months or years. Even in theology and the Christian life that which is considered orthodox and acceptable changes with time, so that cutting edge thinking one hundred years ago may have acquired historical notoriety today.

Humility, and an awareness of our far-from-assured grasp of what may appear assured knowledge, are basic prerequisites in science and theology.

We are limited human beings, and our limitations keep us from pontificating in both areas. In this way we are in a position to dialogue with others, to learn from them, and hopefully to pass on our perspectives to others.

Acknowledging the Centrality of the Mind in the Christian Life

The doyen of English Evangelicalism in the twentieth century, John Stott, was a forthright advocate of the importance of the mind in Christian life. For him, "Christianity lays great emphasis on the importance of knowledge, rebukes anti-intellectualism . . . and traces many of our problems to our ignorance. Whenever the heart is full and the head is empty, dangerous fanaticisms arise."[2] And yet such sentiments are sometimes hard to find among churchgoers.

Being an academic inevitably highlights the central significance of the mind in all our dealings and attitudes. There is no escape from this, and it is one reason why academics can be regarded as strange beasts. If this is true as a general statement, it is doubly true of Christian academics, who can seem to live in a world far removed from that of the ordinary person. This may be accentuated for academics like me who move in theologically conservative Christian circles, where on occasion little space is left for serious intellectual study. This was highlighted in the mid-1990s when historian Marl Noll wrote his epochal study *The Scandal of the Evangelical Mind*, with its devastating opening line: "The scandal of the evangelical mind is that there is not much of an evangelical mind."[3] I would not want to place too much store on aspects of the critique, since it was aimed primarily at American Evangelicalism as he saw it at that time, although a recent update makes many of the same points. Neither does it apply across the board to all conservative scholars, many of whom do not fit this categorization at all. But it does point to a weakness that those like myself have to be aware of, since it provides an important part of the context within which we function.

My basic premise has been that it is essential that we take the world of the intellect seriously and that we strive to ensure that our minds are shaped by God rather than by any of the pressures that bear so forcefully and intransigently upon our thinking and attitudes. This fits alongside my insistence that we refuse to tolerate a secular-spiritual divide in life. Repeatedly, I have

---

2. Stott, "Full Hearts and Empty Heads," 256.
3. Noll, *The Scandal of the Evangelical Mind*, 3.

been known to claim that idealistic and absolutist stances in the reproductive area fail to prepare Christians for the very difficult decision-making that may be required when tragedies or totally unexpected events occur. Unless adequately prepared to think through the complexities and murkiness of the issues, the end result may be willingness to follow the advice of doctors and health professionals coming from a liberal, non-Christian background. This necessitates an ability to weigh up the competing forces in a realistic manner without expecting ready-made answers unable to cope with the tensions implicit in real-life decision-making. Needless to say, this is based on serious thinking and use of the mind.

It is this stance that has led me on a number of occasions throughout this book to accept that the findings of science may provide insight into the ways of God. In the words of Mark Noll, "to accept life in this world as a gift from God, to live as though a deeper understanding of existence leads to a deeper understanding of God, requires dedicated and persistent thought."[4]

While I function within a very contemporary context, it is helpful to reflect that this is not a modern accretion in Protestant thinking. The Puritans in the sixteenth and seventeenth centuries refused to compartmentalize life into religious and non-religious categories. Neither did they exempt non-ecclesial matters from religious scrutiny. For them it was important to attempt to understand the world within a Christian framework. From this it followed that the Puritans were aware of the religious significance of public affairs and the public significance of religious acts.[5] In other words, their thinking was comprehensive and their use of the mind enabled them to think broadly and seek to apply their Christian thinking to all spheres of life and all the areas of daily life they encountered. This did not make them infallible in the whole gamut of their interpretations across every area of society, politics, and science, but their intellectual efforts ensured that their Christian faith was grounded in a highly developed theological framework.

A basic dictum throughout my career has been to love the Lord with my whole mind. Not only has this enabled me to look at the world through a particular set of lenses but also to gain a better appreciation of the works of God. This has never led me to believe in the correctness of all my thinking or interpretations. Far from it. I make as many errors of judgment as anyone else, but it has provided an intellectually challenging framework for which I have always been deeply grateful.

---

4. Noll, *The Scandal of the Evangelical Mind*, 34–35.
5. Noll, *The Scandal of the Evangelical Mind*, 40–41.

This has provided the context and the space for academic debate, intellectual experimentation, and a willingness to accept that traditionally accepted positions may have to be nuanced in light of current knowledge and interdisciplinary perspectives. This is not a given, and I have never been tempted to overthrow numerous traditional positions, but there is no room for naïve and uncritical assumptions when moving in realms for which traditional Christian thinking and biblical insights have no well-grounded directions. And there is a place for input from sources outside Scripture where these sources provide data unavailable in any other way. Christians dare not ignore the actual study of nature, to see how it works, and to understand the intricacies of the world in which we live, and of the bodies that we possess and that make us what we are. For Christians this provides opportunities to glorify God. It is a privilege to understand what makes us what we are as embodied beings.

Much can be learned from reason and experience, even as we interpret the Bible. It is interesting that for thinkers as diverse as Augustine, Bacon, and Galileo attempts to interpret the Bible without employing dialogue between natural and biblical observations guarantees misunderstanding of Scripture.[6] This is another way of saying that Christian thinking needs to take account of two "books": the book of nature and the book of Scripture, with each informing the other—theological revelation and scientific enterprise. These are to be read together, with each contributing to a fuller understanding of the world we inhabit. It was in this manner that leading Protestant theologians and scientists in the late nineteenth century approached contemporary scientific controversies, in particular evolutionary theory. Utilizing their minds, they realized that biblical interpretation needed a contribution from the best science available, alongside which biblical thinking was needed to enlighten scientific conclusions. Anything less dooms one to intellectual superficiality that, in my estimation, is a betrayal of the Christian faith.

A Center for Bioethical Reflection

Many years ago, I was involved in the establishment of the Bioethics Centre at the University of Otago. At that time, I thought seriously about setting up a center outside a university and with an explicitly Christian foundation, as opposed to a secular center in a secular university, inviting contributions

---

6. Noll, *The Scandal of the Evangelical Mind*, 206.

from a wide range of bioethical stances. At that time, it was far from clear which of the two models I should explore. I saw myself as a Christian wanting to educate fellow Christians in bioethical issues. But I also wanted to educate students in thinking bioethically across a wide range of medical and scientific territory regardless of their own worldviews. Since the aim of education is to broaden people's perspectives, by challenging their preconceived notions and stances, presenting them with alternative viewpoints and ways of looking at the world, I concluded that this was where I should place my efforts.

Like many medical academics I was drawn to biomedical ethics not as an observer or interested commentator and hobbyist but as a serious academic pursuit. My aim was to found what may become a world-ranking center of bioethical scholarship in the unlikely geographical location of the antipodes and as a counterpoint to the prevailing Australasian consequentialism that dominated ethical thinking in this part of the world. I did not set out any particular academic approach that would dominate the center, but I did want to embrace those who would undertake searching and scholarly explorations of bioethical issues. This was far removed from any approach that emphasized a certain set of dicta and beliefs to the exclusion of alternative perspectives no matter how worthy in themselves. Nevertheless, I attempted to identify what would move the center forward as an academic and strategic center, calling on a wide array of approaches and expertise beyond the narrowly materialistic utilitarianism found in some centers.[7]

This effort bore fruit in terms of professional acceptability and informed debate on the many issues that confronted twentieth- and twenty-first-century medicine and the biomedical sciences. All along I was committed to attracting to the center those with a broad range of ethical positions rather than any one doctrinaire position, and yet I also sought to remain faithful to my own personal commitments; at no time did I wish them to unduly influence open discussion of the issues. My aim all along has been to embody a spirit of even-handed excellence in areas of scholarship where it is all too easy for emotively-held personal beliefs to hold sway. My background in the more conservative side of the Christian faith has made me aware of the ease with which serious reflection of the evidence (biblically-based in this case) can degenerate into thoughtless commitment

---

7. Many of the thoughts in this section are based on the reflections of Professor Grant Gillett, emeritus professor of bioethics at the University of Otago, given at a *Festschrift* on my behalf on November 27, 2020.

to predetermined and predictable positions no longer open to questioning or modification. Such positions, no matter how well intentioned, isolate them from the wealth of debate circulating within society and prevent them from contributing constructively to that debate. Rather, my aim has been to create a space characterized by an open-ended scholarly spirit, that would, I hoped, benefit the many undergraduate and postgraduate students of all persuasions and cultural identities within the center.

The topics of my own research are many and varied and mirror the ethos of the center. I have sought to open up the many areas in which I have been involved to rigorous academic standards. I have written pieces on dead bodies and our attitudes to them, brain birth and brain death, genetic research, the role of brain function in both scientific and general reasoning, and the impact of scientific innovation on a decent society in which the respect of persons is closely safeguarded. In all of these pieces I have attempted to marshal a diversity of views but always with an unwavering commitment to the unique value of the human being as an organism with special significance, no matter how that may be described.

I have sought to maintain standards that are truly scholarly even when the intended audience is a general, non-academic one. For me, careful scholarship has always been essential, and I have always sought to ensure that any personal opinions of mine do not allow a personal opinion to unbalance an argument and drive towards a pre-ordained conclusion. No matter what the topic, whether clinical practice or underlying biomedical science and its broader implications for society as a whole, I have aimed to be fair to the protagonists and to their case, especially when they have been at odds with my own preferences.

This has meant being quite strident with some Christian students when writing on delicate topics such as PGD. On one occasion, the student in question presented a strongly protectionist viewpoint on the embryo, but then went on to approve of PGD without acknowledging that this entailed the destruction of embryos. As an educator I have no problem with the protectionist position advocated by the student as long as the arguments used are rigorous and consistent. In this case, I would have been happy with an essay arguing against the use of PGD on the basis of a protectionist stance, or approving of it on the basis of a far more liberal interpretation of the value of the embryo. But not a mixture of the two. My own view is irrelevant when it comes to training someone to think ethically, although I would inquire why either a protectionist or liberal position was being favored. In other circumstances, I am prepared to present my own position as long as there is ample room for outlining the reasoning behind my thinking and how it fits alongside competing claims.

Comfortable in the Borderlands

The borderland between Christianity and science is never an easy space to occupy, and it has been incumbent upon me to learn to cope with the tensions inherent in such territory. For many years, I was far from comfortable existing in these borderlands, and I would have been more at home providing answers that I knew Christian groups working with a similar theological framework to me would have welcomed. This would have meant taking positions that were ardently pro-life, anti-abortion, critical of a host of modern technological developments in biomedical areas, and seeking at all times to protect the moral *status quo*. But this was not my path. Although having sympathy with many of these claims, I refused to shy away from what I perceived to be difficult questions and inconsistencies, and I rejected the false comfort of what I considered to be simplistic answers aimed at achieving superficial harmony. I have been prepared to occupy the uncomfortable space of Holy Saturday in between the atoning sacrifice of Good Friday and the triumph of Resurrection Sunday.[8]

Some sectors within the Christian church prefer to hide from modern technology and the advances of science, covering their ears in a theologically-justified Luddism. Others, on the other hand, embrace every technological advance as the source of earthly salvation, embracing a Promethean hyper-agency. Neither of these approaches is helpful, and neither of them provides sustenance for Christians living in the modern world. My aim has always been to work within a theological framework that appreciates both the power of the methodology of science as well as the limitations and distractions of scientism as a philosophy. I have been prepared to admit that we live in a world of broken systems—both biological and social—but that amidst despair there is cause for hope within the creativity and compassion of human persons and the activity of a loving God.

---

8. A phrase used about me by Maja Whitaker, lecturer in practical theology, Laidlaw College, Christchurch, New Zealand, and my research assistant for many years prior to this. This section draws heavily on Dr. Whitaker's contribution to my *Festschrift*, November 27, 2020. Consequently, it provides an observer's view of my approach to bioethics as a Christian.

In grappling with issues within the borderlands, I soon came to realize that I was never going to keep everyone happy. I have consistently raised awkward questions, offered unpalatable answers, crossed partisan lines, and continuously questioned the *status quo* both within and outside the academic establishment. And not everyone has liked it. But for me this is the essence of functioning as an academic; it is about pushing people's thinking, getting them to justify what they believe, why they believe what they do, and what the consequences will be. Not only this, but how strong is the evidence behind our conclusions? Long ago, I came to accept that I may be wrong, I may be misguided, my judgments may be askew; and what applies to me applies to everyone else, including Christians.

When I started writing about the use of unclaimed bodies within anatomy schools and argued for the importance and reasonableness of systems of donation, I encountered considerable opposition. This was not an area in which anatomists were comfortable. But I pressed on, and gradually the tide of opinion changed in my favor. This demonstrates that it is not only churches that cling to well-tried paths. Academics also have their blind spots. But for me this was a path that anatomists should be treading, since it is the outcome of genuine care for the vulnerable and the marginalized who far too often are exploited. When unclaimed bodies are used in the absence of informed consent, this harm does not even end at death. Despite the supposed "necessity" of using unclaimed bodies to ensure a sufficient supply for anatomy schools, I continued to point out that it was nothing less than exploitation of the poor and the vulnerable. This concern for the treatment of the vulnerable reflects the tenor of Scripture and the heart of God for humanity. From my perspective this has been one of my major contributions to ethical thinking, a space occupied by few Christians.

Real People, Real Lives

My approach to ethics has always been rooted in the lived experience of real people—as is evident by the frequent use of narratives (both imagined and sometimes semi-biographical) which appear in a number of my books. I use these examples not so much to reinforce a point or make an argument more memorable (as is often the case) but to illustrate the tensions and difficulties inherent within real-life—whether at the beginning or end of life, at any other edges of life, or the human body once life has ended.

Too often Christian ethics can be abstract and moralizing in a way that is unhelpful for people who are making difficult decisions about their health or reproduction. It is also the territory of sermons (not all of course) where broad principles are extracted from Scripture but little attempt is made to ground those principles in actual real life. What do these principles mean? Where are they leading? What consequences might they have? How is the person in the pew to respond? I am not asking for a definitive "Thou shalt" or "Thou shalt not," but I am searching for sufficient light to be thrown onto what the options might be and the pros and cons of those options.

In the absence of some clear outline of directions, people are left to struggle with unresolved pain as they ask "What should a Christian do?" in this modern situation that the Bible obviously never mentions. Frequently, I have found myself reiterating that there are no easy answers, on occasion to the frustration of some readers and listeners who longed for me to state explicitly that God opposes one procedure or another. For them, the response was simple, and for them any committed Christian was called upon to rail against some new technology or the use of some new resource. The last thing they wanted to hear was a fellow Christian appearing to vacillate. They live in the world of the black and white, while in their eyes I live in the realm of the complex, where so much is grey and murky. I have frequently apologized when this is the case, although for me this is a characteristic of practical theology. It is an approach intended to speak to real people where they come up against disconcerting situations for which there are no neat answers.

Inevitably, much of my work has a strong academic tinge to it. However, I have always aimed to ensure that it speaks to the needs of ordinary people, that it is a pastoral resource that can help everyday people. As an academic I have repeatedly complained about the manner in which some academics are happy to be paid to do what fascinates them but show little interest in public engagement. To make matters worse, universities reward academic staff for acting in this way, and penalize them for "wasting their time" on dubious activities that fail to lead to high-impact publications that by definition generally appeal to a small coterie of academics in their own speciality. This applies as much to ethicists and theologians as it does to scientists. As much as I have indulged in this behavior over the years I have never been content to leave my contribution at this type of academic level and have hoped that I could offer people in difficult situations a compass and a set of guardrails rather than a list of prescriptions and prohibitions.

Dangerous as this approach frequently is, it has seemed to me to be one that aims to takes seriously our joint humanity.

Looking Back

As I look back from many years into the future, at the decision to establish a bioethics center in a secular university, I realize that it said a great deal about me (far more than I could have concluded in the 1980s) and where I stand in the world. I am far more comfortable speaking into secular society from someone within that society than presenting fellow Christians with conservative ethical viewpoints with which they would readily agree. The controversy over *Brave New People* in which I became embroiled in the 1980s also showed me very forcibly that a Christian foundation would have unwritten expectations associated with it, something that would not have worried me over central Christian teaching but that may have proved unnerving in the face of many of the topics with which bioethics has to deal.

This, however, did not mean that I left my theology behind. All my ethical work has a theological grounding even if much of it is not exclusively Christian. Where some in the church, particularly under a certain banner, mourn the end of Christendom—where Scripture supposedly had moral authority in the wider world—I have been at pains to show that moral theology need not be explicitly Christian to bring a Christian influence. There are well-reasoned arguments within Scripture and the systems of Christian thought that can make a helpful contribution to discourse within the public sphere.

Throughout my career I have sought to contribute not only to the accumulation of academic knowledge and the running of universities but also to the running of a healthy and well-functioning society. I have become firmly committed to the notion that we must be committed to the society in which we live, seeking to benefit as many people as possible and not simply a few privileged groups. I accept that my work is often not explicitly theological in the manner in which the field is often characterized, but it is implicitly theological in its approach to human flourishing and our relationships with others and the world.

Some time ago, in a talk I gave to the Christian Medical Fellowship, I stated that I believed I had been called into realms of intense cultural disquiet and that this is where I was to integrate my faith and my learning. This was a conclusion that had taken many years to formulate, and a conclusion that had not been arrived at easily. I have frequently introduced myself as someone whose interests in bioethics are almost entirely in controversial areas. This has never been by choice, and from time to time I have looked longingly at those who can confine their attention to uncontroversial terrain or can deal with issues in such a way that their audiences will applaud their contributions rather than be upset by them. Of course, this depends upon the audience and on the range of audiences one addresses.

Alternatively, I could have remained in neuroscience and found many fascinating highways and byways to explore. That would have been less controversial, although even there I would have continued to explore the brain-mind-soul trichotomy and would have stepped on toes by eliminating the last of the three. But that is another area altogether! As one person expressed it: "I for one am profoundly grateful that Gareth did not refuse this calling [bioethics], discomforted by the difficulties or discouraged by opposition. It would have been easy to hide behind the microscope, absorbed forever in perforated synapses [nerve connections in the brain]; we would, however, have been far worse off."[9]

Living an Integrated Life

A constant temptation for all of us is to think we have the answer—the correct answer and possibly the only acceptable answer. And yet there is much we do not know, and there will be doubts. Whether in science or in theology (or in philosophy or economics for that matter), our understanding is always incomplete, our interpretation may be flawed. We may be wrong. None of this is a challenge to our faith or to the reliability of much in science. There are clear signposts in both domains, but so often those signposts do not provide infallible guidance. After all, we are always functioning within a particular cultural context at a particular time in history. And as individuals we have our own histories, our own limitations, our own prejudices.

Christians do their best, seeking at all times to be led by Scripture and by the Holy Spirit, but this does not allow any of them to know without a hint of doubt that "God said" and that he led them unerringly in this or that precise direction. Neither does science provide "facts" that will never be open to challenge or to be interpreted in alternative ways to those in vogue at the moment. Once again, this does not invalidate the scientific

9. Whitaker, *Festschrift* contribution, November 27, 2020.

method or its extraordinary abilities to change our world and our thinking. Yet again, we may be wrong. Attentiveness to our innate limitations and blunders is crucial.

Human beings are not all-knowing, no matter how able they (we) are. As images of God, humans are privileged creatures, but they constantly fall short and will continue to do so this side of the eschaton. The academic life as researcher and scholar has taught me humility and a profound knowledge of both the temporary nature of all knowledge and the fallibility of all judgments. But it has also shown me the vast opportunities it opens up, and for this I am eternally grateful.

The subtle holding in balance of the realities of life, relationships, points of wonder, and persistent traditions which mold our human dealings with the world and each other means that I have never been drawn into a narrow view that might limit our thinking and cause us to overlook important matters of culture and value. In this I have sought in my own way to capture the wide-ranging scholarship and inclusiveness of the greatest thinkers of today, but I have also sought to speak to the common man and woman whose lives are not influenced by philosophical abstractions. In one sense this is down-to-earth, and reflecting on the dead body with its human uniqueness and dignity only serves to emphasize the earthiness of what we are as human beings. This may appear the last place one would look for the values with which human beings are imbued. Much ethical thinking is limited to biological life and does not encompass that which remains after death, but for me that is an intriguing and ethically challenging question in which we both celebrate and interrogate our conception of human beings and link it to the received wisdom of the ages and to religious strivings. This is where there is an indissoluble link with the divine and, for me, with my Christian conceptions.

Glossary

Assisted reproductive technologies (ARTs): Medical treatment designed to help couples or individuals achieve pregnancy; involves the manipulation of both eggs and sperm; IVF is the best-known example.

Bequeathed bodies (bequests): Bodies donated to anatomy schools for use in teaching and research; as opposed to the use of unclaimed bodies, where there has been no informed consent.

Bioethics: The study of ethical issues in biomedical research and practice; generally considered to encompass medical ethics, where there is a more specific focus on ethical issues in clinical medicine.

Blastocyst: An early embryo at four to five days gestation after it reaches the cavity of the uterus; consists of a sphere of cells with a fluid-filled cavity. Some of the cells (inner cell mass) give rise to the future individual; other cells (trophectoderm) develop into the placenta and support tissues.

Chromosomes: Thread-like structures located inside the nucleus of cells. Each chromosome is passed from parents to offspring, with specific instructions that make each type of living creature unique.

Conception: Equivalent to fertilization; the term frequently used in Christian literature to mark the beginning of human life and personhood.

Glossary

Cystic fibrosis (CF): A progressive, genetic disease affecting a number of organs in the body, but mainly causing long-lasting lung infections. It causes sticky, thick mucus to build up in the affected organs, requiring constant treatment, including hospital appointments.

Embryo: The stage of development from fertilization up to eight weeks gestation in humans, by which point all the major organs have been laid down.

Embryonic stem cells (ESCs): Stem cells derived from the inner cell mass of early embryos (blastocysts). This process leads to the destruction of the embryos.

Epidemic: The rapid spread of disease to a large number of patients within a given population in a short period of time.

Epidemiology: The study of how diseases occur in different groups of people and why; epidemiological information is used to plan and evaluate strategies to prevent illness and as a guide to the management of patients in whom disease has already developed.

Fertilization: The act of rendering gametes capable of further development; begins with contact between spermatozoon and ovum (egg), leading to their fusion, that stimulates the completion of ovum maturation.

Fetus: The developing human being from the end of the eighth week of gestation until birth.

Gene: A unit of DNA in a chromosome; the biological unit of heredity.

Gene editing: An illustration of genetic engineering in which DNA is inserted, deleted, modified or replaced in the genome of a living organism. These technologies can be used on somatic (body) cells (non-heritable) or on germline cells (either for reproduction or not for reproduction).

Genetic determinism: The belief that human behavior and personality are directly controlled by an individual's genes, generally at the expense of a role for environmental factors, whether in embryonic development or in learning.

Gestation: The period of development from the time of fertilization of the ovum (egg) until birth.

Glossary

Intracytoplasmic sperm injection (ICSI): An artificial reproductive procedure involving the injection of a single sperm directly into an ovum (egg).

Inner cell mass (ICM): The cluster of cells in a blastocyst which protrude into the fluid-filled cavity and subsequently develop into the embryo proper and some of the supporting tissues; present at four to six days gestation.

***In vitro* fertilization (IVF):** The process of fertilizing an egg with a sperm *in vitro* in the laboratory and therefore outside the body of the woman.

Induced pluripotent stem cells (IPSCs): Derived from adult skin or blood cells that have been reprogrammed back into an undifferentiated embryonic-like state; theoretically capable of developing into any type of human cell.

Meconium: The earliest stool of an infant resulting from defecation; composed of materials ingested during the time the infant spends in the uterus, including intestinal epithelial cells, amniotic fluid, bile, and water.

Non-invasive prenatal testing (NIPT): A blood test to determine the risk of the fetus being born with a range of genetic abnormalities; analyzes small fragments of DNA circulating in the pregnant woman's blood.

Pandemic: an epidemic of an infectious disease that has spread across multiple continents or worldwide, affecting a substantial number of individuals.

Pederasty: In ancient Greece, this was a socially-acknowledged romantic relationship between an older male and a pubescent or adolescent boy.

Plastinate: Whole bodies that have been plastinated and generally displayed in upright poses.

Plastination: Technique used in anatomy to preserve bodies or body parts, first developed by Gunther von Hagens in 1977. The water and fat are replaced by various plastics, yielding specimens that can be touched, do not smell or decay, and retain most properties of the original sample.

Preimplantation genetic diagnosis (PGD): A procedure to test early embryos for serious inherited genetic conditions; the intention is to transfer only unaffected embryos to a woman's uterus.

Glossary

Rapid antigen test: A rapid diagnostic test suitable for point-of-care testing that directly detects the presence or absence of an antigen; used as a testing method for people with COVID-19 symptoms or household contacts.

Somatic cell nuclear transfer (SCNT): The transfer of the nucleus of a somatic (body) cell of an adult into an ovum (egg), the nucleus of which had been removed.

Stem cells: Undifferentiated cells which can divide indefinitely and in some cases are capable of forming any cell in the body.

Surplus embryos: Embryos created as part of fertility treatment and "left over" once the treatment has finished; they are capable of development, but were not implanted into the woman's uterus because more embryos were created than were ultimately required.

Unclaimed bodies: Dead bodies of humans used in anatomy schools for teaching and research in the absence of any informed consent prior to death, either on the part of the individuals whose bodies are being dissected or their family.

Vaccination: Treatment with a vaccine to produce immunity against a disease. A vaccine typically contains an agent that resembles a disease-causing microorganism and is often (but not always) made from weakened or killed forms of the microbe, its toxins, or one of its surface proteins.

Variolation: Method of inoculation first used to immunize individuals against smallpox with material taken from a patient or a recently variolated individual in the hope that a mild, but protective, infection would result.

Zygote: The product of the union of the male and female gametes at fertilization; a fertilized ovum (egg).

Bibliography

Almughem, Fahad A., et al. "Cystic Fibrosis: Overview of the Current Development Trends and Innovative Therapeutic Strategies." *Pharmaceutics* 12.7 (2020) 616.
Bebbington, D. W. *Evangelicalism in Modern Britain: A History from the 1730s to the 1980s.* London: Unwin Hyman, 1989.
Best, M. "COVID Vaccination and the Church." *The Gospel Coalition Australia Edition*, September 18, 2021. https://au.thegospelcoalition.org/article/covid-vaccination-and-the-church/
Cameron, N. M., ed. *Embryos and Ethics*. Edinburgh: Rutherford House, 1987.
The Cartwright Inquiry. *The Report of the Committee of Inquiry into Allegations Concerning the Treatment of Cervical Cancer at National Women's Hospital and into Other Related Matters.* Auckland, NZ: Government Printing Office, 1988.
Church of England. *COVID-19: The Ethics of Vaccine Certification ("Vaccine Passports"): A Briefing Note,* 2021. https://www.churchofengland.org/sites/default/files/2021-07/COVID-19%20The%20Ethics%20of%20Vaccine%20Certification%20%28Vaccine%20Passports%29.pdf.
Collins, Francis. *The Language of God*. New York: Free Press, 2006.
———. "Science Is a 'Glimpse of God's Mind.'" *Faith and Leadership*, August 30, 2021. https://faithandleadership.com/francis-collins-science-glimpse-gods-mind.
Collins, Nate. *All but Invisible*. Grand Rapids: Zondervan, 2017.
Congregation for the Doctrine of the Faith. "*Instruction Dignitas Personae* on Certain Bioethical Questions." https://www.vaticana/roman_curia/congregations/cfaith/documents/rc_con_cfaith_doc_20081208_dignitas-personae_en.html.
———. "Instruction on Respect for Human Life in its Origin and on the Dignity of Procreation Replies to Certain Questions of the Day." https://www.vatican.va/roman_curia/congregations/cfaith/documents/rc_con_cfaith_doc_19870222_respect-for-human-life_en.html.
———. "Note on the Morality of Using Some Anti-Covid-19 Vaccines." https://www.vatican.va/roman_curia/congregations/cfaith/documents/rc_con_cfaith_doc_20201221_nota-vaccini-anticovid_en.html.

Bibliography

Davis, Pamela B. "Cystic Fibrosis since 1938." *American Journal of Respiratory and Critical Care Medicine* 173 (2006) 475–82.

Deane-Drummond, Celia. "Bodies in Glass: A Virtue Approach to Ethical Quandaries in a Cyborg Age through a Recovery of Practical Wisdom." In *A Glass Darkly: Medicine and Theology in Further Dialogue*, edited by D. Gareth Jones and R. John Elford, 61–79. Oxford: Peter Lang, 2010.

Deer, Brian. *The Doctor Who Fooled the World*. Melbourne, Australia: Scribe, 2020.

Drew, Liam. "Research Round-up: Cystic Fibrosis." *Nature* 583 (2020) S18–19.

Edwards, R. "Reflections on Learning about Morals and Ethics in Biomedicine." *Reprod Biomed Online* 14 supplement 1 (2007) 7–11.

Elford, R. John, and D. Gareth Jones, eds. *A Tangled Web: Medicine and Theology in Dialogue*. Oxford: Peter Lang, 2009.

Goddard, Andrew. *Homosexuality and the Church of England*. Cambridge: Grove, 2004.

Gushee, David. *Changing Our Mind*. 3rd ed. Canton, MI: Read the Spirit, 2017.

Harris, Jim. "Rash Decisions: Anti-Vaccination Movements in Historical Perspective." *Origins* 13 (November 2019). https://origins.osu.edu/article/anti-vaxxer-vaccination-measles-smallpox-jenner-wakefield-immunization?language_content_entity=en.

Hutchinson, Ian. *Can a Scientist Believe in Miracles?* Downers Grove: IVP, 2018.

Hildebrandt, Sabine. *The Anatomy of Murder: Ethical Transgressions and Anatomical Science During the Third Reich*. New York: Berghahn. 2016.

Johnson, Martin H. "Robert Edwards: The Path to IVF." *Reproductive BioMedicine Online* 23 (2011) 245–62.

Jones, David Albert. et al. "A Theologian's Brief on the Place of the Human Embryo within the Christian Tradition, and the Theological Principles for Evaluating its Moral Status." https://research.stmarys.ac.uk/id/eprint/3665.

Jones, D. Gareth. "The Artificial World of Plastination: A Challenge to Religious Perspectives on the Dead Human Body." *The New Bioethics* (2016). http://dx.doi.org/10.1080/20502877.2016.1238580.

———. *Bioethics: When the Challenges of Life Become too Difficult*. Adelaide, Australia: Australasian Theological Forum (ATF), 2005.

———. *Brave New People: Ethical Issues at the Commencement of Life*. 1st ed. Downers Grove: IVP, 1984.

———. *Brave New People: Ethical Issues at the Commencement of Life*. 2nd ed. Grand Rapids: Eerdmans, 1985.

———. "The Changing Face of the Science-Faith Dialogue in a Biomedical Arena." *Perspectives on Science and Christian Faith* 68 (2016) 165–75.

———. "A Christian Perspective on New Zealand's Response to COVID-19." *Perspectives on Science and Christian Faith* 73 (2021) 67–78.

———. "Christian Responses to Challenging Developments in Biomedical Science: The Case of *in Vitro* Fertilisation (IVF)." *Science and Christian Belief* 26 (2014) 137–58.

———. *Clones: The Clowns of Technology?* Carlisle, UK: Paternoster, 2001.

———. *Coping with Controversy*. Carlisle, UK: Paternoster, 1996.

———. "Cystic Fibrosis, Trikafta and Christian Hope." *Stimulus*, July 26, 2021. https://hail.to/laidlaw-college/publication/dVgMOTX/article/6C7nfDA.

———. *Designers of the Future: Who Makes the Decisions?* Oxford: Monarch, 2005.

———. "An Exploration of Religiously-Based Opposition to Clinical and Scientific Interference with the Embryo." In *Reflections in Bioethics*, edited by Jose Antonio Morales-Gonzalez, 169–88. Rijeka, Croatia: InTech Open Science, 2018.

Bibliography

———. "*In Vitro* Fertilization and the Destruction of Embryos." *Perspectives in Science and Christian Faith* 67 (2015) 163–74.

———. *Manufacturing Humans: The Challenge of the New Reproductive Technologies.* Leicester, UK: IVP, 1987.

———. "A Pandemic, Science and Faith." *Stimulus*, May 14, 2020. https://hail.to/laidlaw-college/article/AxfHv3n/.

———. *The Peril and Promise of Medical Technology.* Oxford: Peter Lang, 2013.

———. "The Political Debate on Embryo Research in New Zealand and the Role of Religious Actors and Arguments." In *Religion and Biopolitics*, edited by M. Weiberg-Salzmann and U. Willems, 139–59. New York: Springer International, 2020.

———. "The Public Display of Plastinates as a Challenge to the Integrity of Anatomy." *Clinical Anatomy* 29 (2016) 46–54.

———. "Religious Concerns about COVID-19 Vaccines: From Abortion to Religious Freedom." *Journal of Religion and Health* 61 (2022) 2233–52.

———. "Responses to the Human Embryo and Embryonic Stem Cells: Scientific and Theological Assessments." *Science and Christian Belief* 17 (2005) 199–222.

———. "The Transhumanist Vision: Technological Bliss or Tragic Misadventure?" *Perspectives on Science and Christian Faith* 72 (2020) 95–108.

———. *Valuing People: Human Value in a World of Medical Technology.* Carlisle, UK: Paternoster, 1999.

———. "Where Does New Zealand Stand on Permitting Research on Human Embryos?" *New Zealand Medical Journal* (2014) 127:1399.

———. "The World of Cystic Fibrosis: From Diagnosis to Dignity." In *Theology and the Experience of Disability*, edited by Andrew Picard and Myk Habets, 21–31. London: Routledge, 2016.

Jones, D. Gareth, and R. John Elford, eds. *A Glass Darkly: Medicine and Theology in Further Dialogue.* Oxford: Peter Lang, 2010.

Jones, D. Gareth, R. Gear, and K. A. Galvin. "Stored Human Tissue: An Ethical Perspective on the Fate of Anonymous, Archival Material." *Journal of Medical Ethics* 29 (2003) 343–47.

Jones, D. Gareth, and R. J. Harris. "Archeological Human Remains: Scientific, Cultural and Ethical Considerations." *Current Anthropology* 39 (1998) 253–64.

Jones, D. Gareth, and B. Telfer. "Before I Was an Embryo, I Was a Pre-Embryo: or Was I?" *Bioethics* 9 (1995) 32–49.

Jones, D. Gareth, and Maja I. Whitaker. "Anatomy's Use of Unclaimed Bodies: Reasons Against Continued Dependence on an Ethically Dubious Practice." *Clinical Anatomy* 25 (2012) 246–54.

———. *Speaking for the Dead: The Human Body in Biology and Medicine.* Farnham, UK: Ashgate, 2009.

Jones, David W. "To Bury or Burn? Toward an Ethic of Cremation." *Journal of the Evangelical Theological Society* 53 (2010) 335–47.

Le Peau, Andrew T., and Linda Doll. *Heart. Soul. Mind. Strength.* Downers Grove: IVP, 2006.

Lewis, C. S. "On Living in an Atomic Age (1948)." In *Compelling Reason: Essays on Ethics and Theology*, edited by Walter Hooper, 115–21. London: Collins, 1996.

Luther, Martin. "Whether One May Flee the Plague." In *Luther's Works, Vol. 43: Devotional Writings II*, edited by Jaroslav Jan Pelikan, Hilton C. Oswald, and Helmut T. Lehmann, 119–38. Philadelphia: Fortress, 1999.

Bibliography

MacKellar, Calum. *The Image of God, Personhood and the Embryo*. London: SCM, 2017.

Masson, Victoria, "Why Is Eyam Significant?" *Historic UK*. https://www.historic-uk.com/HistoryUK/HistoryofEngland/Why-Is-Eyam-Significant/.

Messer, Neil. *Respecting Life: Theology and Bioethics*. London: SCM, 2011.

Mouw, Richard J. *Restless Faith: Holding Evangelical Beliefs in a World of Contested Labels*. Ada, MO: Baker, 2019.

Myers, David G. *Psychology*. 10th ed. New York: Worth, 2013.

Noll, Mark A. *The Scandal of the Evangelical Mind*. Grand Rapids: Eerdmans, 1994.

O'Donovan, O. *Begotten or Made?* Oxford: Clarendon, 1984.

Olson, R. E. "The Joker/Jester Asks 'Why Chosen'?" *Patheos*, December 20, 2021. https://www.patheos.com/blogs/rogereolson/2021/12/the-joker-jester-asks-why-chosen/

———. "The 'Ultimate' and the 'Penultimate': An Important Distinction in Christian Ethics." *Patheos*, March 28, 2020. https://www.patheos.com/blogs/rogereolson/2020/03/the-ultimate-and-the-penultimate-an-important-distinction-in-christian-ethics/.

Parsons, Chris. "Vaccine Resistance Is Not New." *Stuff*, November 25, 2021. https://www.stuff.co.nz/opinion/127072550/vaccine-resistance-is-not-new.

Peters, Ted. *Playing God: Science, Theology and Ethics*. Aldershot, UK: Ashgate, 2003.

Peterson, James. *Changing Human Nature: Ecology, Ethics, Genes, and God*. Grand Rapids: Eerdmans, 2010.

———. *Genetic Turning Points: The Ethics of Human Genetic Intervention*. Grand Rapids: Eerdmans, 2001.

Piper, John. *Coronavirus and Christ*. Wheaton: Crossway, 2020.

Pride, David. "Viruses Can Help Us as Well as Harm Us." *Scientific American*, December 1, 2020. https://www.scientificamerican.com/article/viruses-can-help-us-as-well-as-harm-us/.

Ramsey, Paul. *Fabricated Man*. New Haven: Yale University Press, 1970.

———. "Shall We Reproduce? 1. The Medical Ethics of *in Vitro* Fertilization." *Journal of the American Medical Association* 220 (1972) 1346–50.

———. "Shall We Reproduce? 2. Rejoinders and Future Forecast." *Journal of the American Medical Association* 220 (1972) 1480–85.

Richardson, Ruth. *The Making of Mr Gray's Anatomy*. Oxford: Oxford University Press, 2008.

Shaw, Ed. *The Plausibility Problem: The Church and Same Sex Attraction*. London: IVP, 2015.

Sommerville, Troels. "Covid-19: Vaccine Mandate Protesters Force Kids' Cricket Match to Be Abandoned." *Stuff*, December 4, 2021. https://www.stuff.co.nz/national/127188571/covid19-vaccine-mandate-protesters-force-kids-cricket-match-to-be-abandoned.

Stone, Lyman. "Christianity Has Been Handling Epidemics for 2000 Years." *Foreign Policy*, March 13, 2020. https://foreignpolicy.com/2020/03/13/christianity-epidemics-2000-years-should-i-still-go-to-church-coronavirus/.

Stott, John. "Full Hearts and Empty Heads." In *Authentic Christianity: From the Writings of John Stott*, edited by Timothy Dudley-Smith, 256. Downers Grove: IVP, 1995.

Trivedi, Bijal P. *Breath from Salt: A Deadly Genetic Disease, a New Era in Science, and the Patients and Families Who Changed Medicine Forever*. Dallas: BenBella, 2020.

Verhey, Allen. *Reading the Bible in the Strange World of Medicine*. Grand Rapids: Eerdmans, 2003.

Bibliography

———. "What Makes Christian Bioethics Christian?" *Christian Bioethics* 11 (2005) 297–315.
Warnock, Mary. *Report of the Committee of Inquiry into Human Fertilisation and Embryology*. London: Her Majesty's Stationary Office, 1984.
Whiteway, Eleanor, and Denis R. Alexander, "Understanding the Causes of Same-Sex Attraction." *Science and Christian Belief* 27 (2015) 17–40.
Wilson, Ken. *A Letter to My Congregation*. Kindle edition. Canton, MI: Front Edge, 2014.
Wright, N. T. "Christianity Offers No Answers about the Coronavirus. It's Not Supposed To." *Time*, March 29, 2020. https://time.com/5808495/coronavirus-christianity/.
———. *God and the Pandemic, A Christian Reflection on the Coronavirus and its Aftermath*. London: SPCK, 2020.
Yamada, Shigehito, Mark Hill, and Tetsuya Takakua. "Human Embryology." *InTech Open*, October 21, 2015. https://www.intechopen.com/chapters/49200.
Yankaskas, James R., et al. "Cystic Fibrosis Adult Care: Consensus Conference Report." *Chest* 125 (2004) 1S–39S.
Young, Mark, "Recapturing Evangelical Identity and Mission." In *Still Evangelical?*, edited by Mark Y. Labberton, 46–65. Downers Grove: IVP, 2018.

General Index

abortion, vii, 13–17, 21, 69, 82, 83, 95, 97, 99, 105, 109, 121, 128, 148, 155
ACART, 114, 116, 125
anatomy (school), 21, 23, 24, 26, 27, 155, 164
    in Nazi Germany, 24, 28–30
Anatomy Act (1832), 30,
anti-abortion, 15, 17, 97
anti-vaxxers, 59, 61
anonymous archival material, 23
Augustine, 160

Bacon, 160
Bebbington quadrilateral, 6
Best, Megan, 68
Bible, 8, 69, 111, 147, 149, 152, 156, 160, 165
    trustworthiness of, 66
Biblical tradition of lament, 41
bioethics, viii, 2, 10, 25, 96, 115, 155, 161, 167
(bio)medical science (research), 7, 15, 16, 42, 46, 52, 56, 66, 88, 95, 96, 100, 107–109, 118, 129, 156, 161
Black Death, 52
blastocyst, 102–105, 111, 113, 131
body (dead), 29, 100, 162, 168
    body bequests, 24, 29, 31, 32, 33
    body donation, 33
    intrinsic value, 31
    public display, 37, 38
    resurrected, 37
BodyWorlds, 34
Bonhoeffer, Dietrich, 19
brains for dissection, 23
Brave New People, 13, 14, 166
Bush, George W., 124

Carnegie embryo collection, 100
Cartwright Inquiry, 23
Child, gift from God, 80
Christian Medical Fellowship, 166
CMDA, 121, 122
Collins, Francis, 42, 49, 59, 66, 86
Collins, Nate, 146
conception, 15, 83, 95, 108–110, 125
conspiracy theories, 62
controversy, 13
COVAX, 74
COVID-19, 40, 43, 47, 49, 50, 53, 54, 58, 60, 63, 67, 68, 70, 72, 73, 128
    COVID vaccines and mandates, 14
Creation in God's image, 44
cremation, 32, 35
CRISPR, 2
cystic fibrosis (CF), 43, 76–94
    as a disability, 93
    CF gene, 82, 85, 86

General Index

cystic fibrosis (*cont.*)
    costs of drug treatment, 89, 90
    cystic fibrosis transmembrane regulator (CFTR), 77, 85, 87, 88

Dignitas Personae, 108
dissection (human), 26, 27, 30, 32, 111
    and poverty, 30
divorce, 17, 120, 143, 145, 148
Donum Vitae, 108

Edwards, Robert, 100, 123
embryo, 15, 22, 83, 84, 95, 95–97, 102, 103, 107–109, 112, 113, 115, 117, 123, 126, 128, 130, 131, 155, 162
    embryonic stem cells (ESCs), 98, 102, 121, 124
    environment of, 105, 120, 130, 131
    inviolability of, 16, 98, 108, 109, 119, 126
    in vitro embryos, 100, 127
    protection of, 115, 116, 124, 126
    research on, 18, 96–99, 104, 108, 114–117, 119, 123, 125, 128–130
    surplus, 18, 105, 119, 121, 122, 126
epidemiology, 42, 45, 48, 75
equality, 31
Evangelicalism, 7, 14, 19, 142, 158
evolutionary humanism, 3, 4, 66
Eyam (Derbyshire), 45

fertilization, 95, 98, 99, 102, 103, 106, 110, 126
fetus, 15, 22, 83, 99, 103, 112
freedom of expression, 71, 84

Galen, 27
Galileo, 160
gene technology, 10, 79, 85, 119, 128
Goddard, Andrew, 144, 145
God's judgment, 40
Good Samaritan, 48, 74, 107
grave robbers, 28
Gray, Henry, 28, 29
Gray's Anatomy, 28
Grounds, Vernon, 19
Gushee, David, 141

Hildebrandt, Sabine, 25
homosexuality, 134, 136, 137, 144–146, 151
    reparative therapy, 134
    revisionists, 140–145, 149, 150
    traditionalists, 139–141, 144–148, 150
human community, 11
human person, 103, 111, 162
humans as images of God, 12, 55, 103, 111, 113, 124, 168
human dignity, 38, 113, 118, 168
human life as gift from God, 112
humility, 9, 12, 19, 123, 157, 168
Huxley, Julian, 3

Idol (worship), 67, 90
Induced pluripotential stem cells (IPSCs), 103
informed consent, 23, 28, 30, 31, 33, 37,
InterVarsity Press (IVP), 13
IVF (*in vitro* fertilization), 2, 14, 16, 18, 82–84, 96–101, 104, 108, 114–119, 121–123, 125, 132, 144

Jenner, Edward, 60
joker/jester, 154

Lewis, C. S., 55, 56
LGBTQI, 139, 140, 142, 145, 147, 150
life expectancy, 11, 62, 78, 86
Lloyd-Jones, Martyn, 5, 6
lockdown measures, 44, 48, 58, 59
Luther, Martin, 44–46, 67,

MacKellar, Calum, 107, 119
Māori skeletal remains, 22
Mather, Cotton, 60
medical school, 3–5, 28
medical technology, ix, 10, 11, 48, 52
    as an idol, 52
mind, 4, 75, 158–60
misinformation, 59, 60, 62, 73
MMR vaccine and autism, 61, 62
Mompesson, William, 45
Mouw, Richard, 18, 19
moral complicity, 23, 106

General Index

National Institutes of Health (NIH), 43
natural disasters, 43, 50
neighbor love, 48, 49, 51, 65, 70, 74, 113
New Zealand, 48, 114, 116, 124, 125
Noll, Mark, 158, 159
NIPT (non-invasive prenatal testing), 93

one-issue advocacy, 15
opposite sex attraction (OSA), 135, 138
Oxford University/AstroZeneca vaccine, 58

pandemic, 40, 43, 46, 48–50, 52, 55, 56, 59, 68, 70, 71, 75
Pernkopf, Eduard, 29
Pfizer/BioNTech vaccine, 58
plague, 44, 45, 66, 67
plastination, 34, 35, 37
PGD (preimplantation genetic diagnosis), 16, 82–84, 96, 98, 104, 114, 115, 119, 122, 162
playing God, 125
prenatal life, 97, 111, 112, 130
providence of God, 56, 81, 90
pro-choice, 96, 97
pro-life, 15, 16, 96–98, 125, 163
public health measures, 44, 45, 48, 51, 53, 54, 56, 75
public square, 114–19, 124, 126, 128, 159, 166
Puritans, 159

Ramsey, Paul, 108
Reformation, 6, 35
reproductive technologies, 95, 98, 99, 108, 112, 122, 124, 155
    ART (artificial reproductive technology), 121
    commercialism of, 123, 124
respect for body, 32, 33, 36
reverence for human life, 110

sacredness (sanctity) of human life, 16, 34, 109, 110
same-sex attraction (SSA), 17, 133–38, 141, 146, 148–151
    disputable matter, 143, 146, 151

scientific basis, 135–39
science (scientists), 9, 28, 48, 49, 53–56, 58, 66, 72, 73, 75, 85–87, 89, 90, 92, 94, 120, 123, 136, 155–157, 163
    distrust of, 65
    gift from God, 43, 49
    in service of God, 51, 81
science-faith (debate), 14, 16, 18, 42, 49, 65, 69, 89, 118, 139, 151
scientism, 8, 163
Scripture, 8, 18, 19, 29, 49, 69, 129, 145, 148–151, 156, 160, 164
service of others, 44
Shaw, Ed, 146
smallpox, 60
social distancing, 46
Sodom and Gomorrah, 139
SCNT (somatic cell nuclear transfer), 103
Stone, Lyman, 51
Stott, John, 158
suffering, 10, 11

theological ethicists, 12
transhumanism, 53
Trikafta, 87, 88, 90, 92

unclaimed bodies, viii, 22, 24, 25, 29–31, 37, 164
University College London (UCL), 1, 4
University of Otago, 21

vaccines (vaccination), 44, 48, 49, 52, 54, 57–59, 62, 63, 67–72, 106, 128
    and the vulnerable, 64, 65, 68, 70, 73, 74
    legislation, 61, 68
    resistance to, 60, 67
vaccine mandates, 58, 59, 61, 64–67
    opposition to, 64, 65, 71, 73
variolation, 60
Vatican, 68, 108, 130
Vesalius, Andreas, 27, 28
Vinci, Leonardo da, 27
viruses and viral infections, 43, 47, 51, 63

General Index

Wakefield, Andrew, 61, 62
Warnock Report, 128
Whether One may Flee the Plague, 45
Whittenburg, 45

Wilson, Ken, 141, 143–145
Wright N. T. (Tom), 41, 55, 56, 71,

Young, J. Z., 5

Scripture Index

OLD TESTAMENT

Genesis
1:26–27	110
4:1	111
9:6	110
16:2	111
19	139
23:3–18	35
25:9	35
29:31, 32	111
30:22, 23	111
35:19–20	35
35:29	35
49:31	35
50:13	35
50:22–26	29, 35

Exodus
13:19	29, 35
16:1–36	81
20:13	110

Leviticus
18:22	139
20:13	139

Deuteronomy
31:6	47

Joshua
24:30	35

Judges
19	139

Ruth
4:13	111

1 Samuel
25:1	35

1 Kings
2:10	35

Scripture Index

Job
10:3–12	111

Psalms
6, 10, 13, 22	41
8:5–8	62, 89
91:1–2	41
139:13–16	111, 112

Ecclesiastes
11:5	132

Isaiah
40:31	51
49:1	111

Jeremiah
1:5	111
29:7	50

Amos
2:1–3	29, 35

NEW TESTAMENT

Matthew
7:1–5	17
7:16–20	90
14:12	35
22:37–39	74
27:57–61	29

Mark
12:29–31	44, 51, 74, 90
15:42—16:2	29

Luke
1:41–44	111
10:25–37	32, 48, 74
13:1–5	54
18:17	8, 157
18	133

John
4:1–26	32
5:1–18	18
7:53—8:11	18
9:1–41	89
11:17–18	35
15:13	47
19:38–42	35

Acts
11:27–30	55
8:2	35

Romans
1:26–27	139
7:18–19	17
8:18–25	44, 51, 86
10:1–4	3, 4
12:1–2	75
14–15	143–145
14:1–23	151

1 Corinthians
6:9	139
6:19–20	110
8:1–13	67, 151
13:12	9, 157
15:20	37
15:42–52	29

Galatians
5:13–25	84

Colossians
1:17	50
2:16	151

1 Thessalonians
4:13–18	29

1 Timothy
1:10	139
4:1–16	151
5:3–16	81

Scripture Index

Hebrews
2:6–8   89

James
1:27   90

1 John
3:12,15   110

Jude
7   139

www.ingramcontent.com/pod-product-compliance
Lightning Source LLC
Chambersburg PA
CBHW051927160426
43198CB00012B/2066